A COMED

GR

MANOS THE GREEK

McKnight & Bishop Ltd
Laugh

About the Publisher

McKnight & Bishop are always on the lookout for great new authors and ideas for exciting new books. If you write or if you have an idea for a book, email us: **info@mcknighbishop.com**

Some things we love are undiscovered authors, open-source, crowd-funding, Amazon/Kindle, social networking, faith, laughter and new ideas.

McKnight & Bishop Laugh is an imprint for standup comedians helping to get their brilliant ideas to print. Visit us at: **www.mcknightbishop.com/laugh**

ISBN 978-1-905691-27-2

A CIP catalogue record for this book is available from the British Library

First published in 2015 by McKnight & Bishop Laugh, an imprint of:

McKnight & Bishop Ltd.
28 Grifffiths Court, Bowburn, Co. Durham, DH6 5FD
http://www.mcknightbishop.com
info@mcknightbishop .com

This books has been typeset in
Palatino Linotype, Gill Sans MT and Diogenes

Printed and bound in Great Britain by Lightning Source Inc, Milton Keynes
The paper used in this book has been made from wood independently certified as having come from sustainable forests.

Contents

Prologue

This book is Manos's candid account of historical, geographical and cultural aspects of his mother country and its inhabitants. It looks at among other things some important Greek places and islands, its neighbours, the numerous Greek institutions and the grip of the Greek Orthodox Church on Greek society. It will not tell you everything you need to know, and it will certainly not tell you how to get from one place to another. It will, however, give you some interesting and funny facts about Greece, and hopefully help you understand the Greeks a little better. It aims to give you a lot of trivial, inside information about Greece and the Greek culture, as well as a good laugh.

This book is based on the three stand-up comedy shows Manos performed across the UK the last few years namely 'Everything You Always Wanted To Know About Greece But Were Afraid To Ask', 'The Tale Of An Immigrant' and 'Greekonomics'. The performances were in a quest to educate the British about Greece and increase the quantity and quality of British tourists going to Greece. They have had a negligible effect so far, but you can never lose hope. Maybe the answer is a DVD.

Most of the information is painfully accurate, some a mixture and other stuff is just made up because it sounded funny (mostly what is contained in the speech bubbles). Hopefully, you can tell which is which, if not try to find out. It will help you at parties and will satisfy your curiosity.

Greece And The Greeks

What is Greece and what is to be Greek? This is not an easy question to answer, but I thought I would start with the difficult issues. Greece and Greek-dom has a history of more than 5,000 years, so the concept of Greek-ness has changed a bit over the years. There are as many views of what it is to be Greek as there are Greeks. This is my own attempt to explain Greek-ness.

Let's start from the name. It is ironic (Greek word) that the country that gave thousands of words to the world, has the world describing it with the wrong word. 'Greece' in English, 'Grĕce' in French, 'Griechenland' in German, 'Grecia' in Italian. They are all wrong. 'Greece' and 'Greek' are actually Latin words for an obscure little area of Greece, which does not even exist anymore. The word 'Greece' does not even have good connotations for us Greeks as it relates to 'obedience'. In some languages there is a completely different name for Greece which derives from 'Ionians' one of the four ancient Greek tribes. Hence in Turkish Greece is called 'Yunanistan' and 'Yunani' in Indonesian.

The correct names are Hellas (sometimes Ellas) or Ellada (for Greece) and Hellines or Ellines (for Greeks). Hellines according to our history/mythology were the sons of Ellin, the son of Deukalion (who was the son of Zeus) and Pyrra. So there you have it: we are descendants of our supreme God. The name Ellin itself comes from the word Helios (the life giving sun). Now you know why we don't get sunburned easily.

You will find the name 'Hellas' and 'Hellenic' on stamps and on the names of many organisations such as the 'Hellenic Post Office', but officially even the Government uses the words Greece and Greeks, to every Hellin's disappointment. In order to avoid confusion that's what I will use in this book as well, but hopefully I've made my point.

> When Greek people talk about Europe they automatically exclude Greece, but when foreigners talk about Europe Greeks take offence if Greece is excluded.

What is Greek-ness (Hellenism)?

Freedom is the word mostly associated with Greece and it is embedded in our flag which has nine stripes – as many as the syllables of 'Eleutheria I Thanatos' (Freedom or Death) the slogan used during in our nation-defining revolution against the Ottoman empire in 1821.

Freedom from people of other nationalities telling us what do (especially Germans telling us we have to obey fiscal rules). Also, freedom from people of our nationality telling us what to do, we never listen to our Government (especially when they tell us to pay more taxes). It may sound a bit strange but if you knew our Governments, you would probably do the same.

Freedom even sometimes from logic (Greek word). Who needs logic when you have Greek passion? Greeks are not robots, the thinking goes. We have warm blood in our veins so we can behave as we like.

Freedom from silence. We love a loud chat and a heated debate. It can be about life, death or the correct amount of olive oil in the salad. Normally it is about politics – there is always an election coming up. Lately most debates are about the economic crisis. At the end of the loud, heated and animated debate all is forgotten, no hard feelings (usually). We, Greeks love to talk and that's why we invented philosophy (Greek word) a form of talking about thinking.

Freedom from fear of speaking one's mind, the famous Greek outspokenness. We are outspoken to the point of being rude, but we hate it when other people are not polite to us. Hypocrisy is a Greek word and sometimes a Greek trait.

Freedom from loneliness. We hate doing things alone even when no more than one person is required. Company is good and having other people around is a perfect way to have someone to get the better of. To live alone, to us Greeks is alien. To go on holiday alone, unthinkable. People who go on holiday alone acquire a status of a leper. So if you are in Greece on your own right now reading a book, why not pretend that 'all your friends' that you came on holiday with are back in their hotel rooms sick with food poisoning. You'll get some sympathy rather than a pitiful look. Pretending you are on holiday with other people has the additional benefit that people will not think you are on a sexual adventure (unless you are in Mykonos – in which case you are in for a sexual adventure (or read the wrong tourist brochure).

Freedom from fear of death. We know that we are all going to die, so why wear seat belts or helmets that mess up your hair? Let's make the best of life (and our hair). Or even better, let's make a song and dance about it.

Two songs I believe express how we see being Greek, here is a rough translation:

The Truth is One

The Truth is one, there is no immortality.
(and) Even the valley of paradise is not big enough for Greece
My God, I wish you were a drinker to save humanity
(I wish) you got drunk and you knifed Death
Let's all wish St Peter gets ill, so we live for another year.

This one is normally sung by Giorgos Dalaras, our 'national' singer, our own Cliff Richard but with more wrinkles if you like.

The other song, which in my view expresses exactly what being Greek is about, first sung by Giorgos Aggelopoulos, a gypsy by origin, a fact that demonstrates the inclusiveness of Greek society (something we are in danger of losing these days).

Ellinas Eimai Anatolitis
(I am Greek, a child of the East)

I am Greek, an eastern man, born of Aphrodite
A Child of 'Eros' and 'Love', saint by day, rebel by night
I am Greek; don't judge me by the rules of logic
(If you want) to learn who I am, you need to get into my heart
I am Greek and proud, I never regret things I do
A child with 'filotimo' and weaknesses
always looking for opportunities

Being Greek is also about love for your country, your family, food and love itself. Greekness is about friendliness, good intentions and generosity. Above all to be Greek is to feel proud and lucky to be Greek and to be living in Greece itself.

Reasons why Greek people consider themselves lucky:

- Because they are Greek.
- Because they live in Greece.
- Because Greece is a place other people dream the whole year of coming to.
- Beautiful Greece has a beautiful sea and the best beaches.

- Because they speak the Greek language, the richest in the world (factually correct).
- Because watermelon in Greece is bought whole, not in slices.
- Because the Greek diet is rich in olive oil, feta and ouzo.
- Because ketchup is not used in Greece cuisine.
- Because being Greek they can appreciate the sound of bouzouki (a very annoying sound to most other Europeans).
- Because Greece won the Euro 2004.
- Because of ancient Greece and the ancient Greeks (every Greek thinks of himself as a mixture of Socrates and Alexander the Great).
- Because Greece has not conducted any major offensive wars, so not many people resent Greece.
- Because when Greece was building Parthenon the other European nations were still in the forests gathering mushrooms or painting themselves red and blue.
- Because Greece can always borrow more money.
- Because Greece is a small country but Greek people have a big heart (which may explain the high rate of heart disease in Greece).

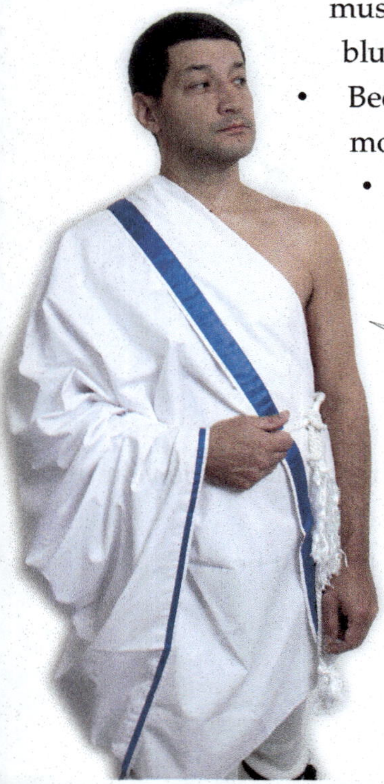

IF (a Greek version)

IF you can keep your head after 15 ouzos
when all about you are drunk and losing theirs
and blaming it on the ouzo,
IF you can trust yourself when all men doubt you,
But make allowance for their doubting too;
IF you can't wait and jump the queues
And feel no shame or being lied about, you out-lie the others,
Or being hated, by your creditors don't give way to hating the creditors,
And yet look very good, and talk very wise:
If you can dream - and not make dreams your master;
If you can think - and not make thoughts your aim;
IF you can meet with Disaster
And treat it like a Triumph (Greek word);
IF you can bear to hear the truth you've spoken
Twisted by the Turkish to make a trap for tourists,
Or watch the world you gave your Greek words to, ungrateful,
And stoop and make new words:
IF you can love and make love your winnings
And not give about money or work a toss,
and lose, and start again at your beginnings
And never breathe a word about your loss;
IF you can force your heart and nerve and sinew
To serve your turn long after they are gone,
And so hold on when there is nothing in you
Except the Will which says to them: "Hold on!"

IF you can resist logic, with no good reason,
Or walk with Kings - nor lose the common touch,
if neither foes nor loving friends can hurt you,
IF all men count with you, except the Turkish
but one too much, except the tourists;
If you can fill the unforgiving tourist
With sixty seconds' worth of distance run,
Yours is the Earth and everything that's in it,
And - which is more – you are a Greek, my son!

You Know You're Greek When...

1. You're 5'4", can bench press 325 pounds, shave twice a day, but you still cry when your mother yells at you.
2. Your mechanic, plumber, electrician, accountant and travel agent are all blood relatives.
3. You have a relative that has done something really bad.
4. You have a relative with connections to the government.
5. Your two best friends are your cousin and brother-in-law's brother-in-law.
6. All your cousins are named after your grandfather.
7. You are on a first name basis with at least 8 waiters in your town.
8. If someone in your family grows beyond 5' 9", it is presumed his mother had an affair.
9. At some point in your life, you've been a waiter.
10. You spend all major holidays with your family irrespectively of your age especially New Year's Eve.

11. Your grandmother/mother/aunt has a miracle cure for every ailment under the sun.
12. You can name any or all of the gods on Mount Olympus.
13. Your mother or father still feels the need to discipline you in public irrespective of how old you are.
14. You can dance Greek dances without music.
15. You must name your children after your parents, grandparents, or in-laws.
16. You have at least five Marias, nine Dimitris, five Nikos, six Georges and four Yiannis in the family.
17. You are constantly told by your parents, 'I am telling you this for your own good'.
18. When you come back from college you still have to live with your parents, and fight over curfew all over again, as if you never left them before.
19. You always curse at Greeks but when you travel you only make Greek friends.
20. You get married to get your freedom from your parents and because you want to prove you are not homosexual.
21. You go out 3-4 times per week even if your income does not allow it, because 'you only live once'.
22. You go to church at Easter (even if you are an atheist).
23. You laugh, burp and fart loudly with no sense of embarrassment (Ok, a lot of other people do that, too!)

History

Greek history is very long and the side effect is that as a pupil, there is so much to learn; so many dates, so many events. Sometimes especially before exams, I wished I was American or even better a New Zealander.

It is difficult to agree when Greek history actually begins. 706,673 BCE (Before Common Era), Sunday afternoon, could be a good starting point. The discovery of a skull in a cave on the Halkidiki peninsula of Macedonia confirms the presence of humans in Greece that year, proving that Greece was a popular holiday destination even for Neanderthals. Near the skull, archaeologists found remnants of a fire, an indication that the first fire had been lit in Greece thus making winter tourism possible.

The Pre-Classical Era: The signs are good

The first area of Greece to excel in civilisation standards were the islands of Cyclades (Mykonos, Paros, Naxos, Andros, Santorini, etc.) at about 3,000 BCE.

The earliest ever erotic graffiti was found recently in Astypalaia one of the islands of Cyclades. Dr Andreas Vlachopoulos, a Greek specialist in prehistoric (Greek word) archaeology (Greek word) chanced upon a couple of racy inscriptions and large phalluses carved into Astypalaia's rocky peninsula at Vathi. The inscriptions, both dating to the fifth century BCE, were "monumental in scale, and tantalisingly clear." One inscription says: "Nikasitimos was here mounting Timiona." There was only one explanation the archaeologist explained: "By using the verb in the past continuous tense, it clearly says that these two men were making love over a long period of time, emphasising the sexual act in a way that is highly unusual in erotic artwork." Another inscription reads: "For a good time wait by this rock." Interesting? More on Greek homosexuality later.

Soon after, Crete overtook Cyclades (in terms of civilisation, not graffiti). The king of Crete had the title of Minos, hence it's called the Minoan civilisation. Crete became very powerful and waged a war against Athens which they won.

One of the Minoan stories worth telling is the story of Minotaur (the bull of Minos). After he ascended the throne, Minos competed with his brothers to rule. Minos prayed to Poseidon, the sea God, to send him a snow-white bull, as a sign of support. He was to kill the bull to show honour to Poseidon, but decided to keep it instead because of its beauty. He thought Poseidon would not care if he kept the white bull and sacrificed one of his own. To punish Minos, Poseidon made Pasiphae, Minos' wife, fall deeply in love with the bull. Pasiphae had a hollow wooden cow made (the bull would not mate with her otherwise, he had standards, I guess), and climbed inside it in order to mate with the white bull. The offspring was the monstrous Minotaur. At least this was the explanation according to the press release of the Royal family.

Minos and his wife were not best pleased with the baby though as it was rather unfortunate looking, it had massive ears and they did not want him to be King (remind you of anyone?). They decided to hide him away from the people. They invited the Lord Foster of the day, Daedalus, and his son Icarus to build a labyrinth (Greek word, it means maze). In order to feed him they asked Athens to provide seven virgin boys and seven virgin girls (one for each month plus a couple spare). Athens grudgingly agreed as refusal meant war. But one year Theseus, the son of the King of Athens, asked to be sent alongside, and with the help of Minos' daughter, Ariadne (who didn't like her brother) he killed the Minotaur.

On his way back Theseus forgot to fly the white flag as agreed with his father Aegeas, and maintained the black one. When Aegeas saw the flag he thought Theseus had died and he threw himself into the sea. Theseus was very sad to lose his father but he was now the King of Athens which eased his pain.

Crete and the Minoans were destroyed by the huge tsunami that followed the eruption of the massive volcano of Santorini around 1,100 BCE. The Cretans have kept a huge grudge towards Cyclades and Santorini to this day (Cretans rarely forget) which explains the scarcity of ferry boat links between Crete and Cyclades, and Crete and Athens and the very few that do exist always run very late.

The destruction of Crete coincided with the rise of the first civilisation in the Greek mainland. It is called the Mycenaean civilisation after Mycenae, its main centre (Greek word). The era of the Mycenaean civilisation was dominated by the Trojan War, which was a war over the most beautiful woman of antiquity, the Beautiful Helen (wife of Menelaus King of Sparta. She is mistakenly called Helen of Troy in English. When Paris, Prince of

Troy raped (according to some) or romanced (according to others) Helen, all Greeks followed Menelaus across the sea and attacked Troy, another essentially Greek city.

The story (Greek word) of Troy is part of a tragic (Greek word) family story and inspired two of the earliest (and longest) poems in the world, The Iliad (the siege and sacking of Troy) and The Odyssey (the return of Odysseus back to Ithaca) and then the homonymous (Greek word) movie with Brat Pitt in the role of Achilles.

The siege of Troy lasted 10 years despite the heroics (Greek word) of Achilles, one of the greatest ever Greek warriors. The Greeks were about to give up when Odysseus had one of the best ideas (Greek word) ever. The Greeks sailed away to a nearby island and left behind a hollow horse (full of Greek warriors) with the message 'This is a gift to Goddess Athena, please take inside the city – No Greek warriors are kept inside this horse overnight'.

Greeks invented the Olympic Games as a tribute to Zeus at Olympia at 776 BCE. Only naked Greek men were allowed to compete – a paradise for everyone who appreciates the naked male body form. Women were of course very keen to watch the games, for obvious reasons. They would often dress up as men, even grow beards – not difficult for Greek women – in order to sneak in.

That horse was called the 'Doureios Horse' not 'Trojan Horse' as it has become known in English. The offering of the horse gave rise to the saying 'Beware Greeks bearing gifts'. It should be corrected 'Beware Greeks bearing gifts to their enemies'. At night, once the horse was inside the city, the warriors came out of the horse's bumhole (literally) and opened the doors to let the others in. They burned Troy to the ground, and at the same time wrote their own destiny as the escaped Trojans immigrated to Rome which helped give impetus to the establishment of Rome and the birth of the Roman Empire, which conquered Greece later on. Karma on a geopolitical scale or what?

> Hercules is still considered the ultimate bodybuilder and all round strong man. Movies and series (Greek word) are still made about him some 4,000 years later. He was a son of Zeus but Hera hated him as he was born out of wedlock – she was the Goddess of marriage after all. Hercules completed 12 ....er... Herculean tasks on orders from his brother King of Argos, who was a demanding boss. Like many men throughout history and across many cultures, due to the seduction and betrayal of a woman, he died a painful death. He went to heaven to sit next to his father (Greek word), Zeus.

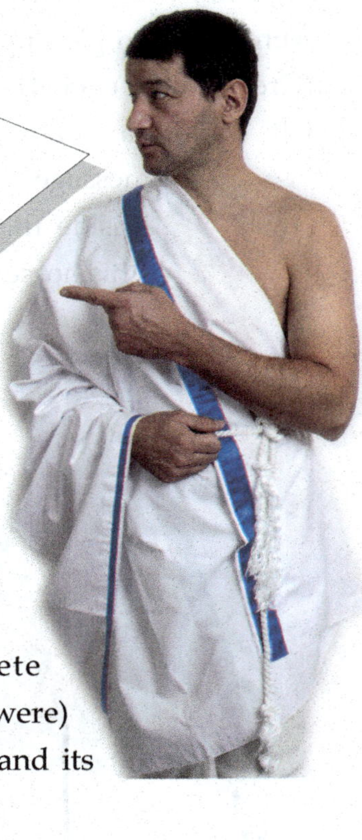

The defeat of Troy led to the complete domination of Greece (good times these were) in the Mediterranean basin (Greek word) and its division to independent 'city-states'. The most famous and populous city-states were Athens, Sparta, Corinth, Argos and Thebes.

The Classical Era: Greece at its best

At around 460 BCE the people in Athens had an idea. Let's stop having someone tell us what to do and let's decide for ourselves. Democracy was invented. No fighting, not a single drop of Greek blood (they saved it for later). Democracy was so cherished and valued that it was not open to every one. No slaves could vote, or women, immigrants or people without property. The reserve of white, male Athenian property owners. Some democracy you may say.

Sparta went the other way; if one is good, two is better. They went with two Kings, a kind of insurance policy.

> "By all means marry. If you get a good wife, you'll be happy. If you get a bad one, you'll become a philosopher" said Socrates.

The Persian Empire decided they didn't like Greece and thought of it as a small annoyance. Democracy was not something they wanted spread about. When the Athenians helped the rebellion of fellow Greeks under his rule, the Persian Emperor Darius found the excuse he wanted and attacked Greece in 490 BCE. The Persian army was massive, some say 250,000, some say one million (Greeks are not very good with numbers). The Athenians asked for help from the Spartans, but when the Athenian messenger arrived to mighty Sparta, Spartans said, "We'd love to help mate, but we are having a 'Moon Festival' this weekend. Let's do war next weekend."

Following the refusal of Sparta to help, the Athenians went to war alone. Although massively outnumbered, 10,000 Athenians beat the Persian Army and drove them out to sea. A Greek soldier, Philipidis, was so excited with this momentous victory that he couldn't wait to tell his mates back in Athens. With mobile phones yet to be discovered he ran 40 km to Athens to bring the news and the gossip of the battle. Alas, he was so exhausted (no Lucozade back than) on arrival that he just shouted, "We f****** won!" and he dropped dead. To honour this sacrifice in the name of news distribution, marathon races are organised around the world to this very date much to the annoyance of the Persians (nowadays Iranians), except in Iran.

Darius died soon after the battle but his son Xerxes wanted to have a go at beating the Greeks. He amassed some one million soldiers from the vast areas of the Persian Empire and thousands of ships, and came to Greece to do battle.

With no 'Moon Festival' planned this time the Spartans were eager to help and gain some glory themselves. They wanted to stop him at Thermopiles (The Gates of Fire). Three hundred of them under King Leonidas vowed to die defending Greece. The rest is history (or more accurately the scenario of the blockbuster 2007 Hollywood movie '300').

"Every non-Greek is a barbarian," is a popular saying in Greek even today. 'Barbarian' is a Greek word and comes from the sound 'bar-bar-bar' which is how foreign languages sounded to the civilised Greek ear. It was not considered such a bad word until some really nasty non-Greek people came round. The statement may be considered racist but it was good racism. Anyone could become a member of the 'higher' race if they learned Greek and adopted good manners, hence improving themselves. "Greeks are those who have Greek education," Socrates a great ancient orator declared. In that respect, ancient Greeks were the perfect racists or elitists if you want.

The Spartans were defeated only after a local shepherd showed the Persians a path to get behind them, but they got the glory (and a movie). Leonidas and his 300 Spartans (as well as, 1,000 other Greeks who rarely get a mention) fought to the death. The Persians destroyed an empty Athens but they lost the big naval battle at Salamis, and the Persian army was obliterated at the Battle of Plataea a year later. Persians lost interest (and face), Greece and Europe were free.

With the Persians defeated and no other enemy in sight the Greeks decided to start fighting among themselves. Athens grew bigger, stronger and richer and with some help from its friends (on whom they imposed heavy taxes) built the Acropolis a wonder of the ancient world. The Spartans got jealous of Athens and its glory and declared war. It was to cost them dearly but eventually they won.

The peace lasted for a while before another round of wars started between the various city-states, which lead the eminence of Thebes.

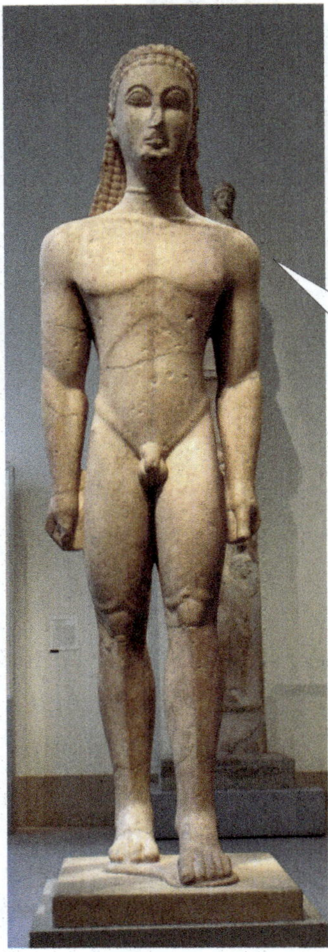

Someone said to Aristippos that his younger wife Laida did not love him; she only pretended to do so. Aristippos answered, "Neither wine nor fish love me but I enjoy them."

This style of statue is called 'kouros'. The size of their penis is in no way indicative of the average ancient Greek penis.

Socrates (469-399 BCE), was widely lauded for his wisdom.

One day an acquaintance ran up to him excitedly and said:

"Socrates, do you know what I just heard about Diogenes?"

"Wait a moment, before you tell me I'd like you to pass a little test. It's called the Triple Filter Test," Socrates said.

"Triple filter?"

"That's right, before you talk to me about Diogenes let's take a moment to filter what you're going to say. The first filter is Truth. Have you made absolutely sure that what you are about to tell me is true?"

"No, actually I just heard about it."

"All right, so you don't really know if it's true or not. Now let's try the second filter, the filter of Goodness. Is what you are about to tell me about Diogenes something good?" Socrates said.

"No, on the contrary…"

"So, you want to tell me something about Diogenes that may be bad, even though you're not certain it's true?" Socrates continued.

The man shrugged, a little embarrassed. Socrates continued, "You may still pass the test though, because there is a third filter, the filter of Usefulness. Is what you want to tell me about Diogenes going to be useful to me?"

"No, not really."

"Well, if what you want to tell me is neither True nor Good nor even Useful, why tell it to me or anyone at all?" concluded Socrates.

The man was bewildered and ashamed. This is an example of why Socrates was a great philosopher and held in such high esteem.

It also explains why Socrates never found out that Diogenes was sleeping with his wife.

The Hellenistic Era: Greekness Goes Global

The 4th century BCE saw Macedonia rise to power firstly with Phillip II, and subsequently with Alexander the Great. Phillip II swiftly conquered the rest of Greece which was too fragmented to put up any meaningful resistance. Following Phillip's death (some say on the orders of his wife Olympia, some say a male lover became jealous of another of Phillip's lovers) Alexander conquered the known world i.e. the Persian Empire, Egypt and parts of India. Partly in revenge for Persia's attack a few centuries earlier, partly as a drive to spread Greek-ness around the world and partly because he wanted to become famous. If the X-Factor was invented in ancient Greece he would have gone there instead probably. I can just hear Simon Cowell's comments:

"No Alexander. You need to do better. Conquer China first and come back next year. Just because you are a King's son you are not getting away with it!"

Alexander succeeded in making Greek the language of the world, and Greekness was something people from today's Greece to India aspired to. He died at the age of 33. If he hadn't the world today would be much more Greek (and less Roman).

Alexander's empire collapsed after his death into many fragments but it left a lasting effect. The period during and after Alexander's death is called the Hellenistic Period, and it's probably the pinnacle of Greek cultural domination over most of what was then the known world. Good ancient times!

THE ROMAN EMPIRE: THE NEMESIS OF GREECE

But it was now the turn of the Romans for empire, and they had little difficulty in conquering and annexing a fragmented (once again) Greece.

It is said that Rome conquered Greece but Greece civilised Rome (a Greek saying). Greek philosophers, poets and writers emigrated to Rome (alongside the looted riches of Greece) where they educated the Romans – at least those who could afford it. Greece, and in particular Athens, benefited from Roman patronage and enjoyed the reputation as the intellectual capital of the Graeco-Roman world. Many of the historical buildings in Athens today were built by Roman Emperors (not literally, it was slaves who did the hard work, as always, in the ancient world).

The Roman Empire split in half by the end of the 4th century CE with a Latin West and a Greek East. They both spoke Greek but the East had a Hellenist culture while the West a Roman one. The establishment of Christianity moved the centre of the Greek world from Athens to Constantinople (Istanbul). The schism of the Christian Church into Catholic and Orthodox completed the split, and the two parts of the Empire went their separate ways.

Things were not bad for the Greeks during the times of Byzantium (Eastern Roman Empire) apart from parts of Greece being occupied by Venetians, Catalans, French, Serbs, Bulgarians, Italians, Goths, Slavs etc. at different times.

The Ottoman Era: The S*** Hits Greece

During the 14th century the nemesis of Byzantium emerged in the area: the Ottoman Turks. They conquered Constantinople in 1453 and the rest of Byzantium soon after. Despite calls for help from the Western Christendom no aid arrived. Greeks never forgot this and a lack of trust towards the 'West' still persists subconsciously (go disprove 'subconsciously' if you can).

The Birth of the Modern Greek State

Some Greeks had it good under the Ottoman Turks but the majority of the population never liked the occupation (who does?) and they kept making trouble but with little effect. After almost 400 years, in March 1821, the Greeks decided that enough was enough and started a proper revolution against the Ottoman Empire. The organisation of the Greek revolution was not great so they ended up starting at different places and at different times, but the whole of Greece was up in arms (not just arms but spades, sticks etc.) against the Ottoman occupier.

In the second year, despite the considerable success of the revolution, it was evident that Greece needed many more guns. Someone had a brilliant idea: Let's borrow some money to buy guns. We can't be a proper country without any debt, anyway.

A committee from Greece went to England and negotiated the terms of a loan (our credit rating was not good back then either, but we had a clean record). We borrowed 800,000 British Pounds, a huge amount at that time. It was good and allowed Greece to get some more guns. But it was addictive so six months later Greece asked London for another loan. This time Greece got two million British Pounds. Out of this 2.8 million the Greek people only ever received 1,094,700! The rest of the money was spent in intermediaries and commissions. Still, we paid the whole amount back in full, the last payment was actually in 2009 and all in all, including interest and fees we gave back 2.3 billion! In 1824, Greece was bankrupt (didn't take long, did it?).

The Greek revolution attracted many foreign lovers of Classical Greece to come and fight for the cause of Greek freedom. The most famous of them all was Lord Byron the English anarchist (Greek word), aristocrat (Greek word) and poet (Greek word). Most Greek towns to this day have at least one road or avenue named after Lord Byron. Byron came to Greece to fight the Ottomans, but he never actually did. He wrote some poetry instead and died after three months on Greek soil from syphilis. But he lent some Greek warlords some money for the revolution and he is honoured for that. Greek people value good intentions, poetry and low interest lending.

In 1827 the Greek revolution was in big trouble, it was losing ground everywhere and was infested with internal troubles. You see, while fighting the Turks, the Greeks had managed to also fight two civil wars! When the Egyptians landed in Peloponnesus to help the Ottomans, the Greek revolution seemed destined to fail like so may others before it. However, Greece was saved with a bit of help from its friends (effectively its lenders, who were afraid they may lose their money). A combined Russian, French and British fleet sailed down to Peloponnesus to press for a ceasefire, but they engaged (by mistake) in a naval battle and destroyed the Ottoman-Egyptian fleet in the Bay of Navarino. Fighting continued until 1829 when the Ottoman Sultan under enormous pressure accepted Greek independence.

The U.S. (land of the free and all that) was one of the last countries to recognize Greece as they were busy being extra nice to the Ottomans. They were after exclusivity rights on Ottoman opium (the best quality opium, before cheaper, Chinese opium became available). For these and many other reasons, such as American support for the military Junta of 1967 and a blind eye towards the Turkish invasion of Cyprus, Greek people do not have the best feelings towards the U.S.

Greece had already elected its first president in 1827. Ioannis Kapodistrias was a good president, but he was assassinated in 1931 by a Greek family who didn't like him. Then followed another intervention by Russia, France and Great Britain, who decided that we should have a King. Apparently democracy was not suited to the people who invented it.

In 1833, the Great Powers installed King Otto, a German teenager from Bavaria who got up the noses of the Greek people, literally from the moment he set foot on Greek land as he stepped first on his left leg, a sign of bad luck in Greece. He gave most jobs to his mates (who happened to be Germans) and they started spending money like it was their own. He introduced the German Penal Code which applies to date and means that you have to prove your innocence to court. On the plus side this system means that there are no strange lists of antiquated laws that someone could infringe unwittingly.

Ten years later, in 1843 the Greeks decided they had enough of King Otto, and demanded a constitution and jobs for the Greek people, to which Otto conceded.

In 1862, the Greeks managed to get rid of the King and the German monarchy in a bloodless coup. So back to democracy for Greece? No, the British had other plans. They offered Greece a present (the Ionian Islands) and at the same time they eased young

Prince William of Denmark onto the throne. A case of 'beware the British bearing gifts'. But he turned out to be a good King, and became known as King George I. He brought much needed stability, good laws and introduced the use of bacon in Greek cuisine. During his 50-year reign Greece staged the Olympic Games in 1896. Because the Greeks are generous and sharing people they allow other nations to stage them every 4 years. Selfishness is not a Greek word.

In 1897 it was time for another war with the Ottoman Empire, a war which Greece nearly lost, but as a condition of the peace agreement, Crete was put into international administration which led to its union with Mama-Greece in 1905.

The 20th Century

In 1912 another war with the Ottoman Empire, but this time Greece got wise. They teamed up with their Balkan friends against the common bully (although by this time the Ottoman Empire was known as 'the sick man of

Europe'). In 1913 Greece and Serbia fought against Bulgaria. Result: Macedonia was again Greek.

In 1921, shortly after the First World War (when Greece took part on the side of the allies, whereas the Ottoman Empire on the side of Germany) it was time for another war with the Ottoman Empire which had now become Turkey. But this time Greece lost spectacularly (partly because the 'Allies' let her down). The effects of that 'Catastrophe' are still evident today. Most towns in Greece have suburbs called 'Prosphygika' meaning 'the refuges' where the refugees expelled from Asia Minor settled after the 'Catastrophe'.

Dictatorship (Greek word) followed dictatorship until the late 1930s (with time for another bankruptcy in 1932), but another fine hour was ahead for Greece. When fascist Italy and Mussolini asked tiny little Greece to surrender the Greek people all answered with one voice: "F*** off!" (OXI in Greek). We actually won the war with Italy (they made some very stupid mistakes) who then asked the Germans for help. They proved too much of a test for Greece. Greeks soldiers fought bravely and cleverly but they lost. As a result Greece lost the war and was divided into three and occupied by Italians, Germans and Bulgarians.

"Greeks don't fight like heroes,
heroes fight like Greeks,"
said Winston Churchill

During the occupation of Greece, Churchill had the brilliant idea of asking the Royal Navy to blockade the Greek ports so no food would get in for the German troops. Some of his advisers pointed out that this would merely inconvenience the German army, who would simply steal the food from the Greek people who would then starve to death. "Well," said Churchill, "death is a good way to escape the Nazis."

But the British people came to our aid. A group of academics and concerned people in Oxford founded Oxfam, who got special permission to start sending supplies to Greece. Because of the blockade a total of two German troops died (because of allergy to fried calamares), as well as 300,000 Greek people. But they died among a lot of Oxfam bric-a brac.

Oxfam, the Oxford Committee for Famine Relief, was set up in response to famine in Greece in 1942.

The Great Famine, as it became known, has had lasting effects. Greeks mums to this day have a fixation with food. The Italians were the better of the occupiers, but cats and dogs became extinct from homes and gardens. 'Fido-Bolognese' and 'Pussy-stew' were popular dishes for the Italian army.

The British wanted to thank us for our contribution to the war, so they gave us a gift: civil war. They manipulated the various Greek fractions, sold guns to both camps and let the Greeks get on with it. We have had much experience in fighting among ourselves, anyway. For Greece the war was over in 1949, but it took until the 1980s for complete national reconciliation. After the war the country was in a political (Greek word) and economic (Greek word) mess, and many Greeks left Greece to spread Greek-ness to other countries such as the U.S., Germany Canada, Belgium and Australia. There are very few countries with no immigrants from the land of Odysseus. Nowadays there are 10 million Greeks in Greece and another 10 million outside of Greece.

During the 1960s the rest of the world had sex, drugs and rock 'n' roll. We had a military junta (blessed by the C.I.A). It was quite brutal (and comical at times) and it came to an end when in an effort to gain public support they tried to unify/annex Cyprus in 1974. Turkey grabbed the chance and invaded a large part of the island which it still occupies to this day.

In 1981, after a couple of right wing governments, the elections brought a socialist government to power. Andreas Papandreou (son of an ex-prime minister) tried to heal the wounds from the civil war and give Greeks something to cheer about: civil service jobs, good salaries and early retirement. He set the mood for the big party.

One factor that led to the development of Greece in the 1980s was tourism. Greece was discovered as a tourist destination initially by gay people (they tend to discover the best places). It all started with Mykonos and then it spread to all the Greek islands. The Greek sun, food and relaxed way of life soon attracted gay and heterosexual people from all across Europe and beyond.

Another cause of the good times was that in 1981 Greece joined the (then) European Community, which was followed by adopting the Euro in 2001.

Greek Euros, minted in 2008.

COMPLAINTS RECEIVED BY TOURIST AGENCIES FROM DISSATISFIED TOURISTS VISITING GREECE

"I think it should be explained in the brochure that the local convenience store does not sell proper biscuits like custard creams or ginger nuts."

"It's lazy of the local shopkeepers in Corfu to close in the afternoons. I often needed to buy things during 'siesta' time — this should be banned."

"On my holiday to Kos, I was disgusted to find that almost every restaurant served Greek salad. I don't like salad."

"I'll book my holiday but only if I can screen my fellow travellers first''

"We booked an excursion to a water park but no-one told us we had to bring our own swimsuits and towels. We assumed it would be included in the price."

"The beach was too sandy. We had to clean everything when we returned to our room."

"We found the sand was not like the sand in the brochure for Santorini. Your brochure shows the sand as white but it was more yellow."

"They should not allow topless sunbathing on the beach. It was very distracting for my husband who just wanted to relax."

"No-one told us there would be fish in the water. The children were scared."

"Although the brochure said that there was a fully equipped kitchen, there was no egg-slicer in the drawers."

"We went on holiday to Greece and had a problem with the taxi drivers as they were all Greek."

"The roads were uneven and bumpy, so we could not read the local guide book during the bus ride to the resort. Because of this, we were unaware of many things that would have made our holiday more fun."

"It took us four hours to fly home from Crete. It took our French co-travellers only two hours to get home. This seems unfair."

"I compared the size of our one-bedroom suite to our friends' three-bedroom and ours was significantly smaller."

"The brochure stated: 'No hairdressers at the resort'. We're trainee hairdressers and we think they knew and made us wait longer for service."

"There were too many Greek people in Greece. The receptionist spoke Greek, the food was Greek. No one told us that there would be so many foreigners."

"We had to line up outside to catch the boat and there was no air-conditioning."

"It is your duty as a tour operator to advise us of noisy or unruly guests before we travel."

"I was bitten by a mosquito. The brochure did not mention mosquitoes."

"My fiancé and I requested twin beds when we booked, but instead we were placed in a room with a king bed. We now hold you responsible and want to be re-reimbursed for the fact that I became pregnant. This would not have happened if you had put us in the room that we booked."

The Economic Crisis

The story of the Greek crisis (Greek word) started in October 2009 when the Socialist Party (PA.SO.K) got elected to government under the slogan 'There is money'. They meant elsewhere. The leader of the Socialists was Giorgos Papandreou, known as Giorgos the Third because he was the third member of his family to be the prime minister of Greece.

Giorgos, wanted to make a fresh start in the rotten world of Greek politics. He rejected Government statistics (Greek word) and conducted an independent review of the budget which showed an annual budget deficit of 12.5%, instead of the previously stated and rather wishful 2%.

Following that the American credit agencies downgraded the credit ability of Greece from AA- to Z+. They did so because they thought that Greece may not be able to pay back its debt, which is flattering really. It means that until then, they thought Greece would. Bless them.

There was no way we could actually pay the debt, because let's face it, in Greece for the last 30 years we had a party. It was a good party based on debt. Great stuff!

I was married when Greece joined the Euro in 2001 and I was very pleased (not with my marriage, with Greece joining the Euro).
Being an economist my Danish wife was suspicious. "Manos," she says looking at the historical figures...
"Greek historical figures? Aah! Socrates? Plato? Demis Roussos?"
"No, Manos, statistical figures," she says (she never understood my humour). "It seems to me the government may have 'massaged' the figures."
"Rubbish. Why do you say that?" Knowing the Greek politicians (who were in charge of the statistics) I had doubts myself, but I thought the EU must have checked the Greek economy. Before you enter into a relationship with someone you check their assets, I did. More importantly, I was married, I was in an argument and I had to win it, so I played the race card.
"You are a racist! You cannot accept that people with olive skin can have a good economy." So I made a profound statement: "Until you apologise, no more sex!"
My libido though did not care about the Greek economy, so to avoid temptation I had to resort to self-abuse. Some people fight for their country, some people die for their country, for my country I masturbated. Some people gave Greece their lives; I gave sperm (which is a form of life, I guess).

Before every election in the 1980s and 1990s, each political party would choose a social group or a profession and promise them early retirement funded by extra loans.

The Greek constitution specifies we should have elections every 4 years, but on average we have them every three years, so most Greek people have ended up on early retirement and numerous other benefits.

580 professions retire early due to unhealthy conditions: bomb disposal experts, coal miners, taxi drivers (outside Attica), hairdressers, barbers, cleaners, cooks, administration personnel (office workers, supervisors and guards), street sellers, till cashiers, trombone players etc. My own brother has been a pensioner since he was 43. He served on the police force for 25 years, retired on full salary and with €40,000 as a 'welcome to retirement' present by the Greek Government. Brilliant!

Small groups were not enough to win elections so before each election, both political parties bribed the wider population with well-paid public sector jobs.

The system (Greek word) of jobs and perks for votes worked for a while, but all good things must come to an end. The party organised by the politicians and the bankers ended, and the Greek people got the bill.

Sweet, innocent Angela Merkel

It was a huge bill; we know how to party. So, what do you do with a huge bill requiring quick payment? Exactly, that's what we did - we passed it on to the Germans! Giorgos went to see Frau Merkel.

Merkel: "Vas ist Das?"

Giorgos: "Aaah, the bill."

Merkel: "But ve make no party!"

Giorgos: "You never do! But you made the war!"

Merkel: "Aah! Ve are very sorry about the war."

Giorgos: "Prove it, pay the bill."

I love the British sensitivity: 'Don't mention the war'. Please do, as long as they feel guilty they'll keep paying.

In our case they didn't. Angela Merkel (known in Greece as The Angel of Death) refused to lend any money to Greece directly. They thought we would treat their loan to us the same way they treated our 'loan' to them. You see, during the occupation Germany 'borrowed' from the Bank of Greece all of the Greek gold. Actual gold. When the Greek Government remembered to ask for it back (sometime in the 1960s) the German Government said it was nothing to do with them.

"It wasn't us who borrowed the money," said the German Chancellor. "It was the Nazis; ask for the money from Adolf Hitler."

"And what nationality was the Hitler?"

"Austrian!"

"OK, fair enough."

The other reason Angela didn't want to lend Greece the money was because some German and other north European voters believe the stereotype (Greek word) that Greeks do not work, which is of course nonsense. Greek people work the longest hours in Europe, more even than the British: 2,119 hours per year compared with 1,390 for the Germans. Yes, I thought that too, Greek statistics. No EU figures, official stuff. We do work an awful lot of hours, though truth be told, when it comes to productivity do rank very low. You see, it is one thing to turn up for work; it's another to actually do any.

And it's also a weather thing. Let's face it; heat makes you lazy, tired and horny. You can't work hard with a hard on. Do you know a hot country with a strong work ethic? The only one that comes close is California, which has been in debt since the 1990s. And what's the biggest industry in California? Exactly! 'Erotic' movies. Maybe there's an idea for a competitive Greek industry. We have some pristine locations, great natural lighting and many willing actors.

After the refusal of Angela to give Greece a direct loan our Giorgos had an excellent idea:

"Hello, Ocean Finance?"

"I am Giorgos from Greece; I have a huge debt and want to consolidate it to an affordable monthly payment."

" … "

"250 billion Euros!"

"Beep, beep"

"Hello, hello????"

Dominique Strauss-Kahn, Managing Director of the IMF, 2007-2011

Finally, after rejecting calls for a Wonga loan, because not even Giorgos was that stupid, he went to the ECB (European Central Bank) and IMF (International Mother F*****s) for help. Here's the actual dialogue (from Wikileaks.org, I swear!):

IMF experts: "Don't panic! We will help you to pay your huge low interest loan."

Giorgos: "Thank you! At last someone who wants to help the Greek people. What should we do?"

IMF: "Not much, simply continue to buy arms, tanks and submarines at high prices from France and Germany and implement the toughest austerity measures possible on the Greek people."

Giorgos: "That's easy. We would do this anyway, that's our job. How will you help us?"

IMF: "We will help you to pay off your huge low interest loan by giving you another loan, but with a high interest rate. We want to help you so much we will give you the biggest loan ever received by any country in the history of Europe!"

(If you think about it, it makes sense. If you have a party, you get drunk and the next day you have a hangover, the best thing to do is to have a few more drinks 'the hair of the dog' - an ancient Greek phrase.)

Giorgos: "That's sounds amazing but we can't pay the first loan, how will we pay the second loan?"

IMF: "With another loan, silly. Next year we will give you a third loan, even bigger, the mother of all loans, in exchange for more austerity."

Giorgos: "That's very generous, but how will we pay back the third loan?"

IMF: "Don't worry, by then all your creditors will be able to see that there is no way you can repay them back so they will forgo most of the debt. You will have a 'haircut' but you will owe the money to us."

Giorgos: "And what's the point of all this financial faffing about?"

IMF: "There is a big point. At the end of all this Greece will be so f****d up that no other country will dare not pay back its debts!"

Giorgos: "Challenging, what's in it for Greece?"

IMF: "Don't be ungrateful Giorgos. You'll be famous again. The whole world will be talking about you for weeks, for months, maybe decades! You will be more famous than your ancestors and you will be bigger heroes than the ancient Greeks. They only had to fight the Persians; you will have to fight unemployment, poverty and hunger. If anyone survives it will be a miracle but think of the fame and glory!"

And that's exactly what happened. If you don't believe me, google it! So, we got the loan, but in doses like a drug. And it is like a drug, it makes you feel good. But after every couple of months the Greek people develop withdrawal symptoms (Greek word), so they send the prime minister to beg for more.

There is only one small problem. In order to keep receiving the loan instalments, the ECB and the IMF wanted to impose practices that in effect would change the Greek lifestyle and national character (Greek word). They wanted us to pay taxes. We can't do that! 'Tax' is not a Greek word!

They say that the more taxes we pay the more money the Government has to spend on us. But if they are just going to spend our taxes on us why can we not do this ourselves? The real problem (Greek word) is that the Government will not spend the money wisely. They will carry on buying expensive French planes (Greek word) that we don't need (factually correct), expensive German submarines that don't steer straight (factually correct) and houses for themselves (factually correct). When you have such a Government, not paying taxes is simply looking after your money. You wouldn't hand a burglar your valuables, would you?

I remember in 1989 my auntie Sofia and uncle Spyros had a massive row about who to vote for, and they tried to get me to take sides.

"Manos do you love me? If you love your auntie and you don't want to see her die from too much work you need to vote for the socialists."

"What are you talking about Auntie Sofia? You will not die from work; you will retire at 58 like every other Greek woman."

"My innocent Manos, if the socialists win the election they will give me an early retirement because I am a hairdresser."

"On what grounds, auntie?"

"On what grounds? The PASOK say I do a very unhealthy job, I am on my feet all day and I handle chemicals. I could die from them. If you vote for PASOK I'll give you 1,000 drachmas (€3, back then, good money)."

"OK, I understand. I'll do it for 2,000 drachmas. A good price because I love you auntie."

1800 drachmas later (haggling), my uncle invited me to a café for a coffee.

"Nephew, I want you to listen to me. Please, I need you to vote for the conservatives so I don't have to work until I die."

"Why uncle? You will retire at 60 like every other Greek man."

"If they win they will give me an early pension because I do a very dangerous job, in a very dirty environment, I could get ill any moment I work."

"But Uncle you are a radio presenter!"

"The Conservatives say that the microphone (Greek word) has millions of bacteria on it, very unhealthy environment. My mouth is on the microphone for many hours every day. It's a miracle I am alive."

"Yes, but it's your own microphone, your own bacteria."

"Don't be smart donkey. I'll give you 2,000 drachmas."

"If you put it that way uncle, I'll do it for 3,000."

So I got 4,800 drachmas richer and voted for the communists. It's called democracy (Greek word).

After a month of performing my free comedy show at the Edinburgh Fringe I managed to collect a sizeable amount of donations towards Greece: £7.86!

HOW THE GREEK CRISIS DID NOT SPREAD AROUND THE WORLD:

'Spain is not Greece'
Elena Salgado, Spanish Finance Minister, Feb 2010

'Portugal is not Greece'
The Economist, April 2010

'Greece is not Ireland'
George Papakonstandinou, Greek Finance Minister, Nov 2010

'Spain is neither Ireland nor Portugal'
Elena Salgado, Spanish Finance Minister, Nov 2010

'Ireland is not in 'Greek Territory'
Brian Lenihan, Irish Finance Minister, Nov 2010

'Neither Spain nor Portugal is Ireland'
Angel Gurria, Secretary-General OECD, Nov 2010

'Italy is not Spain'
Ed Parker, Fitch MD, June 2012

'Spain is not Uganda'
Mariano Rajoy, Spanish PM, June 2012

'Uganda does not want to be Spain'
Ugandan Foreign Minister, June 2012

I hired a couple of handymen to do some work done in my house in London. The plumber was called 'Spongy', a very appropriate name, I thought. He was a very nice guy until the moment I asked for a receipt.
A receipt? Why do you want a receipt?? What have I done to you?
Despite 20 years in Britain I cannot get used to the freezing/boiling water taps. He installed the mixer tap, but it kept leaking.
"Hey Spongy can you fix the mixer tap."
"Mr Manos, relax. You have to accept things, it is what it is."
"Yes, it's leaking!"
Then I told Russell the plasterer (also receipt allergic):
"Please don't make a mess; you're making the house really dusty."
"Mr Manos, we're all dust. We come from dust and we go to dust."
I thought I hired two law-abiding, British handymen. I got two friendly, tax-dodging philosophers. I felt at home!

The most worrying development is that the crisis has turned many Greeks into Nazis. In 2009 an ultra-nationalistic, racist, neo-Nazi party emerged: 'Golden Dawn' (sounds like a type of fetish club). Golden Dawn is anti-Turkey anti-Euro, anti-Muslim, anti-Jewish, anti-EU, and anti-gay (like the British UKIP but more honest). Like UKIP they are also anti-politics, which is rather strange. If you are anti-politics you don't form a political party, you stay out of politics. You don't go into prostitution to protect your virginity.

They sometimes distribute free food to homeless people (but only if they provide evidence of their Greek identity). They have been guilty of beating immigrants, fighting with protesters, even the murder of a singer (the trial is ongoing in late 2014). Despite their antics (Greek word) they took about 10% of the votes in recent elections. And 10% voted for the Communists making 1 in every 5 Greek voters an anti-democratic fruitcake. This is a sad development for the birthplace of democracy (Greek word).

Golden Dawn is openly racist and it's very difficult to be racist in Greece. It is difficult and confusing to hate people with slightly darker skin than you. Everyone in Greece gets dark in the summer, so Greek racists have to stay indoors, rubbing whitening toothpaste onto their skin. Sales of Colgate have rocketed.
The irony is that to keep their skin white, when Golden Dawn members go out they wear a 'burqa'.

If you walk alone in Athens and you have very dark skin you may be approached by a few mean-looking guys in dark clothes, asking questions about your identity. Don't worry. Just say 'Heil Hitler' and they will let you go on your way. Greek racists can be friendly.

Zakynthos is a Greek island popular with tourists. Before the crisis, out of the 41,000 inhabitants 4,500 were officially registered as 'blind'. When the crisis hit Greece the government asked them to go for a re-examination, A miracle happened; 4,499 people found their sight! God exists; He lives in Zakynthos and cures blind people.

Despite the dire economic situation, the Greek Government refuses to tax the property of the ever powerful and rich Greek Orthodox Church because 'you cannot tax God, he is everywhere'. If we had the 12 Greek Gods we could tax them heavily as they were Greek residents, not domiciles for tax purposes!
It is worth knowing that the salaries of the Greek Orthodox priests are paid by the Greek Government (i.e. the few Greek taxpayers).

POSSIBLE SOLUTIONS TO THE GREEK CRISIS:

- Some have suggested that we could sell the Acropolis; it's got to pay for itself they say (but the majority are against this).
- Britain could help. They can give us some money and keep the Acropolis Marbles legally (there is little chance of getting them back anyway).
- Alternatively, the German Government could give us some money for the war reparations we never received (because they never paid), or they could give us back the Greek gold they 'borrowed' during the war. Fat chance of that I reckon, too.
- Tourism is another possible way out of the crisis. The Greek Tourist Organisation has organised a campaign to bring more tourists to Greece with a very imaginative slogan: 'Come to Greece'. They paid €2million for that.

- There is only one realistic solution: Copyright on all Greek words. Every time someone uses a Greek word (unless he is Greek of course) he pays a penny. With 56,186 Greek words in the English language alone Greece will be minted in no time.

Advantages of the Greek crisis for Greece:

Today's generation has its own myth (Greek word). My grandfather's generation used to say, "I fought in the war and survived." My father's generation used to say, "We fought the military junta and survived." The young Greeks of today will be able to say, "I fought the IMF and put the pictures on Facebook!"

Greek people used to argue about who is going to pay the bill at the end of dinner for hours (- I pay, -No I pay, -I tell you I pay, - No I pay.....). Now if they ever go to dinner, when the bill comes they talk French to the waiter, they blame the Germans and they go Dutch. We have turned into Europeans.

When you have a coffee and you leave a 20 cent tip the waiter looks you in the eye and says 'thank you'. Before the crisis with a Euro tip he'd give you a look like you killed his mother.

You go shopping in Greece and there are no queues. There's nothing on the shelves either but I am trying to be positive.

Every Greek has become an expert in financial issues. War teaches the Americans geography, the crisis teaches Greeks economics.

Greek coffee shops are full of unemployed scientists with at least two post-graduate degrees. You go to have a coffee and talk a bit of football and you end up discussing black holes.

The Greek national animal: the donkey. Beautiful, friendly and always willing to give tourists a ride (I mean this in a nice way).

Geography

Greece and the countries north of its border are collectively known as 'The Balkans'. You may have heard of the Balkans because of Ratko Mladic 'The Butcher of The Balkans' or previously because of Slobodan Milosevic also known as 'The Butcher of the Balkans'. That is the problem with the Balkans: we eat too much meat.

ALBANIA

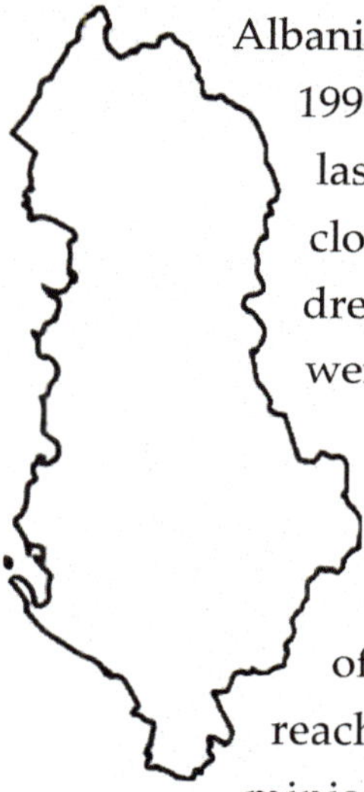

Albania lies to the northwest of Greece. Until the 1990s, Albania was a very backward country, the last communist regime in Europe. Its borders were closed to all foreigners (the kind of country UKIP dreams about). The Albanian people lived like they were in the 1700s, and Albanian's biggest contribution to Greek life was to provide us with the shortest joke: Albanian tourist.

All this changed a few years after the collapse of communism in Europe (like everything else it reached Albania many years later). In 1991 a Greek minister (Antonis Samaras) had the bright idea to challenge the country to open its borders to the world. The Albanian prime minister took up the challenge and opened the borders: within weeks about one million Albanians (50% of the country's population) entered Greece, which they considered paradise (Greek word).

Indeed, they discovered things they never knew existed: coffee, rice and TV.

Paradise: 'Para' means money, 'dise' means give. The place where they give you money.

They soon realised though, that in order to have all these things you need money, and despite the fact you can actually take money from 'holes-in-the-wall' (cashpoints to you and me), you must first work and earn it. When reality hit home, half went back to Albania.

Nowadays, the 400,000 Albanians who live and work in Greece are well integrated and provide much of the manual labour needed to do all the jobs Greeks don't want to (or cannot) do. They are often blamed in the Greek press for higher crime rates, unemployment and heavy rain – just like immigrants everywhere these days.

F.Y.R.O.M. (SKOPJE)

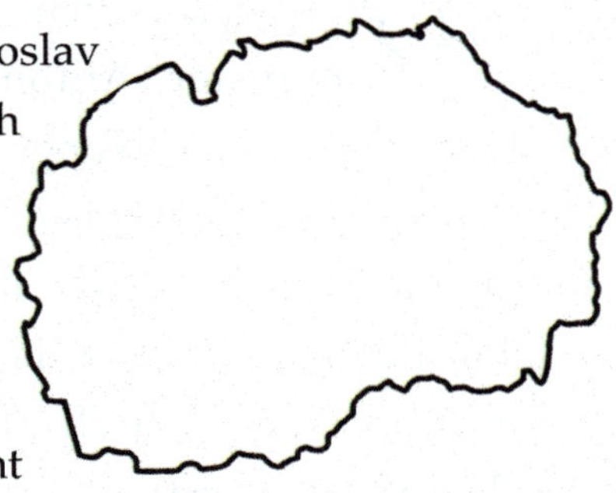

F.Y.R.O.M. stands for Former Yugoslav Republic of Macedonia, which indicates the problem. Macedonia is a Greek word, and although Greeks do not normally mind other people borrowing their words, in this instance the Government decided to take exception. Imagine if France, for example, wanted to adopt the name Britain for one of its provinces? (OK, bad example).

Given that one of the most famous Greeks of all time, Alexander the Great, was from Macedonia, the majority of Greek people support the government in their insistence that FYROM changes its name. Needless to say, in true Balkan fashion over 20 years later the problem is still not solved.

BULGARIA

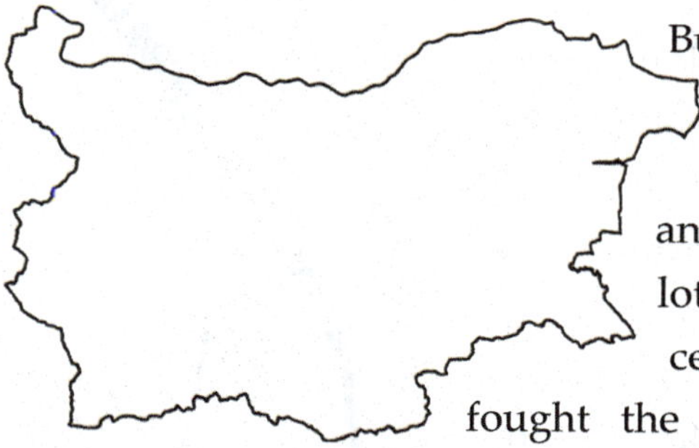

Bulgarians arrived in the neighbourhood around 700 CE (Common Era). Greeks and Bulgarians used to fight a lot, but in the last couple of centuries they have jointly fought the Turkish a couple of times instead. It is difficult to understand Bulgarians (who go mental from time to time) but they are largely harmless. They remind me of a crazy neighbour who mostly minds his own business but from time to time will come and crap on your lawn. He will then carefully collect his shit and apologise. Bulgaria is famous for the absence of any kind of cuisine. What they eat is a mystery.

TURKEY

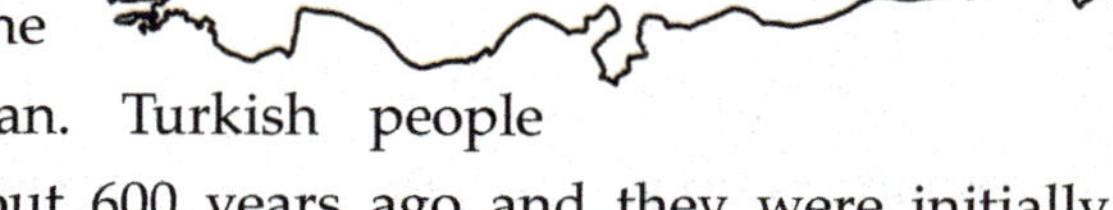

Turkey (or as we call it 'Occupied Greece') lies to the east of Greece, and it is the eternal bully of the southeast Mediterranean. Turkish people arrived in the area about 600 years ago and they were initially known as Ottomans.

"Turkey is a country of 75 million fools ruled by a handful of very smart people, while Greece is a country of 10 million very smart people run by a handful of fools" goes a popular Greek saying.

There remain many unresolved issues: Turkey wants half of the Aegean Sea, half of Cyprus and for Greek coffee to become Turkish coffee again. Although the concept of Turkey is detested, despite the stereotypes most Greeks don't hate the Turkish people, and when left on our own we have lived side by side peacefully. We share food, dance and music tastes after all. It's the governments we vote for that 'make a mountain out of a molehill' (a phrase of Greek origin) and ignite nationalism whenever there are internal problems that need sorting out. But Greece has one over on Turkey, we were crowned Europeans Champions in 2004, they were not!

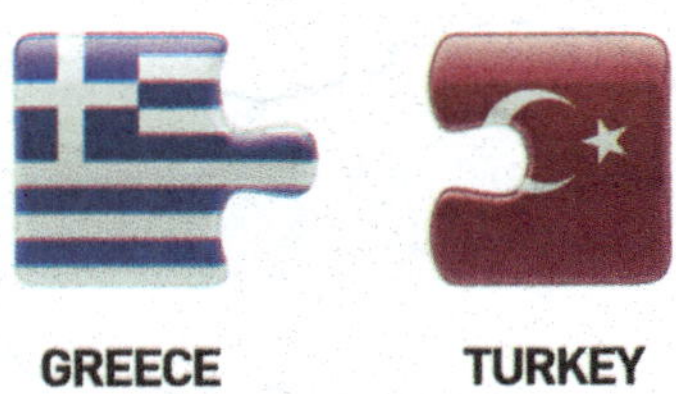

How Turkey sees its relationship with Greece

How Greece sees its relationship with Turkey

Personally I like the Turkish people. A new neighbour recently moved in next door. His name is Ahmet but I affectionately call him Saddam. He moved in a few months ago together with his wife, his six kids and his beard. So I did what any reasonable person would do in my position. I called the Anti-Terrorist Unit!

Most interesting places in Greece

Greece is full of interesting places and it is rich in history (collectively known to foreigners as 'tourist info').

Athens

A great city, home to 50% of Greece's population. Affectionately known by the rest of the Greeks as 'The Bog' due to the uncleanliness of some parts, created by the fact that a population of five million live in a space that can comfortably accommodate about ten people.

As far as many Athenians are concerned 'Athens is Greece and Greece is Athens'. This attitude has created much animosity and even hatred amongst the rest of the Greek people.

The Acropolis

The Parthenon

Athens is home to the Acropolis and the Parthenon, the epitome of ancient Greek Classical art, a magnificent temple to the goddess

Athena. It may not look completed, but in fact the Parthenon and the rest of the Acropolis was finished on time and on budget (something we cannot say about the 2004 Athens Olympics), but it was destroyed during the bombardment by the Venetian navy in 1687, when they were fighting the Ottomans. The Venetian General Franscesco Morozini The B*****d looted Acropolis of its large sculptures.

The final disaster for the Acropolis came in 1801-1812 when Lord Elgin the B*****d, 'removed' most of the remaining marbles. The 'Acropolis Marbles' stolen by Lord Elgin the B*****d is a sensitive issue for every Greek because:

- Some people try to justify Elgin's actions by saying he had a permit from the Ottoman Sultan. So can Greece buy Big Ben from the Germans?
- Many people call them the 'Elgin Marbles'. They are not Elgin's! If Jack burgles your home and steals your TV you'd be annoyed if people started calling it 'Jack's TV?'
- The stolen marbles are not hidden away (so we could potentially forget about the whole sorry affair) as it is common practise for stolen goods but exhibited at the British Museum for everyone to see. Talk about rubbing salt into the wound.

- Why is it called 'The British Museum'? There is nothing British in it! It contains mostly stolen art crafts from India, Egypt and Greece.
- A recent campaign by the British museum recently used the slogan 'Come to the British Museum for a sense of Ancient Greek Art'. Yeah, right. You mean a sense of Modern British Kleptomania (Greek word).

On the plus side, the 'removal' of the marbles destroyed Elgin financially. Goddess Athena punished him well!

I urge every reader to buy his marbles from legitimate sources. My mate Stavros has some excellent original specimens if you're interested.

During the Cold War in the 1950s Piraeus (the port of Athens) was the base of 10 US naval ships including 2 aircraft carriers and 3 submarines. They were based there in order to safeguard the western world from a possible Soviet invasion. With a big number of American sailors around the port, a sex industry quickly developed, and Piraeus attracted prostitutes from all over Greece. American sailors paid well. The lack of condoms led to a very large number of illegitimate children. Greek society accepted these children, and nowadays they are fully integrated in to society. They still live mostly in Piraeus and they all support Olympiakos Football Club, hence the popular slogan 'Olympiakoi, Poutanas Gioi (Fans of Olympiakos, sons of bitches'. I support Panathinaikos FC!

Thessaloniki (or Salonika)

The second largest city in Greece is Thessaloniki, where the people have a funny accent, so a kind of Birmingham-by-the-sea if you like. Seriously, the people of Thessaloniki are the most self-centred of all Greeks, and that's a lot of self-centrism. They have a victim mentality, they are paranoid and feel under constant persecution from the 'Athenian Establishment' which they are, deservedly.

They support various mediocre football teams, mostly PAOK (pronounced BAOK). If you ever go there – not a popular tourist destination, unless you are Russian – tell them you hate Athens and Olympiakos FC. They will be buying you drinks all night.

> 'It's all Greek to me' does not apply in Greece, for obvious reasons. Greek people understand Greek. 'It's all Chinese' is the Greek equivalent.

Crete

The biggest island in Greece, so big that in many places it does not feel like an island at all. Crete to Greece is what Texas is to the US, and what Yorkshire is to the UK: a place with its own laws. People keep guns and they can be less than welcoming to foreigners (their definition of 'foreigners' includes other Greeks, too).

Nikos Kazantzakis (1883-1957) is a famous Cretan writer. Two of his novels have been turned into Hollywood movies: Zorba the

Greek and The Last Temptation. He was considered for a Nobel Prize in literature but it didn't happen following pressure from the Greek Government, (who in turn had bowed to pressure from the Greek Orthodox Church), as they thought some of his writings were anti-church (which they were, for good reason).

Kos

A beautiful, yet somewhat dry island. Like most Greek islands it is full of history (Greek word). Kos's most famous son is Hippocrates (Hippocrates translates to 'he who holds the horses'). He was born in 460 BCE and established scientific medicine as we know it. When Hippocrates first started curing and healing people, he didn't charge any money, he relied on donations. "How can you ask money from a sick person?" he argued. An early one-man-NHS you may say.

It was in Kos that the ancient Greeks first cultivated lettuce. Hence even today the main variety of this calorie-free leafy plant bears its name (i.e. Kos lettuce).

LESVOS

A beautiful green island, famous for its olive oil. It is also the birthplace of lesbianism (Greek word).

No one knows who discovered lesbianism but it was probably a woman. What we know from historical sources is that lesbianism thrived in the court of Sappho, the most famous daughter of Lesvos. She wrote poetic poems (Greek word) for young women who worshipped her; she was a celebrity of her time. Like Madonna but more of a woman. Lesbianism started as a hobby, and for the first few years it was open to men. But that soon stopped as it was deemed to be against the spirit of lesbianism. Some historians have argued that the emergence of lesbianism was made easier by the sexual practises of Greek men who were interested in other Greek men (and who can blame them, have you seen the statues? Greek men were gorgeous!)
At the height of lesbianism in the 3rd century BCE the whole of Lesvos was inhibited by lesbians. There was not a single man on the island! The absence of men led to the discovery of dildos, which proved very popular.

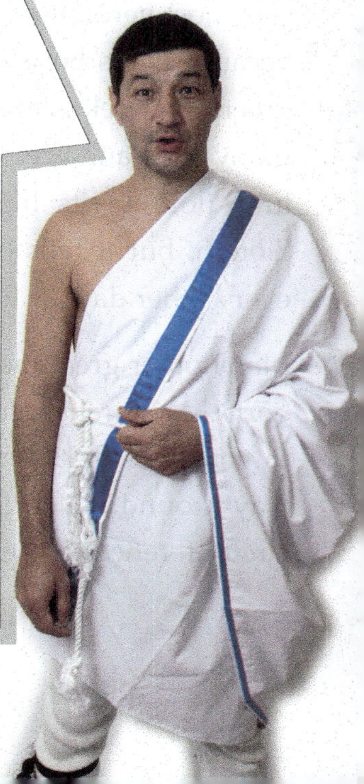

A woman with a dildo painted on a vase, c. 490 BCE

SAMOS

The most verdant and beautiful of the east Aegean islands, I know because I was born there some 30 years ago. Samos is one of the greenest Greek islands. The actual island is soily brown, but with many trees and greenery on it, it looks green from afar. It owes the lush flora to its high rainfall. Samos has the same rainfall as Slough, but it falls only during the 4 winter months rather than every other day (as it does in Slough).

Many other great men have been born in Samos (where I was also born). Aristarchus, for example, was the first ancient philosopher to conclude that the earth moves around the sun, not the other way round. Not only that but he estimated the earth's circumference to the kilometre. But, of course it was Copernicus and Galileo, who re-discovered that eons (Greek word) later and got all the glory.

Samos was the first place where humans made wine according to historical records, at least in Europe. Ironically, King Angaios of Samos who planted (or rather his slaves did) the first acres of vines and made the first ever wine, never tasted it. One of his slaves cursed him never to do so because he was too harsh with the slaves during the planting of the vines. And so it happened. As Angaios lifted his cup to drink the first sip of wine, he received news that a wild hog was destroying the fields. He died trying to kill the wild animal. Served him right.

Pythagoras is another famous son of Samos (the island where I was born). He established trigonometry (Greek word) maybe as a way to get his own back on the schoolchildren that mocked him. Pythagoras was a religious man and established an esoteric religion called 'Pythagorianism'. He demanded his disciples avoid eating beans, because beans cause fart-ness. He believed every time you fart you lose a little bit of your soul. He never farted himself (but then again he always kept things to himself). Ironically, beans were the cause of his death. When pursued by his enemies he had two options: to cross a field of beans with a good chance of escaping, or go around it and meet certain death. He was man of his beliefs and chose death. Legend has it that as Pythagoras took his last breath under the knife he simultaneously let rip a long, loud fart, which almost choked his killers.

Nowadays, Samos (where I was born), is a popular tourist destination. It is famous for its rich flora and fauna with over 3,435 species of plants and animals (which is exactly the number of native species to the British Isles, amazingly). Every year it is visited by tourists from all over Europe, mostly Germans. Every spring you can see hordes of them along the roadsides and mountain paths, inspecting the native flowers for symmetry and the local animals for virility. Many Germans have bought old run-down houses (at the asking price, no haggling, nothing, are they stupid?) and ex-barns, which they do up as summer houses.

Please note, the people of Samos are not called Samosas!

Did I mention I was born in Samos?

I left Samos for the UK because I am a fan of the Anglo-Saxon model of life: study hard, work hard, get a mortgage, work even harder, pay off mortgage, die!

GREEK SOCIETY

RELIGION

In the ancient times, Greece used to have its own religion, pretty much like every other nation. The Greeks are religious people; even atheists in Greece are religious. Ancient Greeks used to worship 12 Gods, namely Dias (or Zeus) and his relatives. The ancient Gods were fun and very permissive. Basically (Greek word), it was like the country was run by teenagers with superpowers.

Zeus was the father of all humans and Gods. To be more precise he was father to some, brother to some others and lover to the rest as a lot of the time he could not keep it in his pants. Whenever he would see someone he fancied (he favoured tall, busty brunettes), he would come down from Olympus where all Gods lived and suggest a quickie (he didn't do long term relationships with mortals as he was already married to Hera and busy running the world). Most girls were happy to oblige (he was great looking), but some were a bit reluctant, in which case he would transform into an animal (a bull, eagle or swan mostly) or even rain, and have sex with them.

Hera was his elder sister and wife (stop judging, they were Gods). She was born in Samos and was the goddess of women and marriage, which is a bit ironic (Greek word) as her husband was the most adulterous of all Gods. She was very jealous and usually she would punish the women who slept with Zeus – even those who did it without knowing whom they were doing it with. Her favourite animal was the peacock (not sure how relevant it is but I thought to mention it).

Athena was a daughter of Zeus. She was born out of his head (don't ask, he was God, he could do anything he wanted). She was a militant virgin and the Goddess of wisdom. Think Ann Widdecombe but younger, pretty, non-homophobic, non-Catholic, non-Tory and wise. So the opposite of Ann, I guess. She was reading all the time and in her later years, she wore glasses. Her favourite animal was the owl (not exactly the wisest looking animal). If she was alive today she would be the Goddess of books. She was the protector of Athens and she had the best ever temple dedicated to her, the Parthenon (Greek word, means Virgin-atory)

Artemis was the Goddess of hunting. She was also a virgin, but not fanatic about it. She was just waiting for the right God, hence she took out her frustration on the poor animals. If she was alive today, she would support fox hunting and whale hunting (not sure about the latter as whales are not living in Greek waters). She was the twin sister of Apollo who was gorgeous and the God of music and harmony. Today he would be a hippie.

Hades was the God of the Dead, and not very happy about it. He was more about taking care of the dead than causing death to the living. Nowadays he would be a Goth.

Demetra was the Goddess of farming and earth. If she was alive today she would be doing all her recycling and running about with Greenpeace.

Aphrodite was the Goddess of love and sex. The statue of Aphrodite of Milo can testify to her perfect breasts. Considering it is over 2,000 years old, it's a miracle they are still so perky. Today she would probably be the Goddess of Soft Porn.

Hephaestus was the son of Hera following a self-insemination (like aphids), partly to take revenge on Zeus for all his affairs. He was so ugly as a baby that Hera threw him down from the heavens and he broke his leg. He was good at making and repairing stuff. Zeus married him to Aphrodite for a joke. Today he would be the God of DIY and worshipped at B&Q every weekend.

Aries was the God of war and he loved fighting. Since he was a God he was always winning. When he didn't make war he made love. At some point he hooked up with Aphrodite (the ultimate coupling of beauty and testosterone). It didn't end well because her husband Hephaestus found out and made a bed-trap for them and paraded them naked in front of the other gods. Did Aries care? Not a bit.

Poseidon was a brother of Zeus. Have you seen the movie 'The Poseidon Adventure'? Nothing to do with the God. The only common thing between them is the sea, as Poseidon was the God of the sea. He protected all sailors (at least those who did not die, anyway).

Dionysus was a liberator. He liberated people from themselves by getting them drunk. He was the God of wine and an alcoholic himself. He could drink as much as he wanted with no risk of liver damage, a kind of British superhero. He was good fun and used to run about with a group of loose women having a heck of a time and many orgies.

Hermes was another son of Zeus (in revenge for the self-insemination of Hera). He was very clever and cheeky so he was made God of Commerce.

Nowadays, 96% of Greek people – at least in theory – follow the Greek Orthodox Church, a very traditional arm of Christianity. On closer inspection one could argue that certain religious festivals have changed little since the ancient times, and the old set of Gods have just been replaced with a new one.

God Zeus was replaced with Simply God who is somewhat less sexy, much older looking and his son Jesus took the place of Apollo. In Greece, Jesus is pictured almost as good looking as

Apollo but significantly less interested in music and women. The Virgin Mary took the place of Athena and Poseidon was replaced by St Nikolaos who now protects the sailors from the sea, and the sea from oil tanker spills. St George is our modern Hermes and St Dimitrios (St Jim to you and me) is the protector of the Greek Army, like another Aries.

The Council Of Gods by Raphael, c.1517

FASTING

Fasting features a lot in the Greek Orthodox Church calendar, 40 days before Easter, 40 days before Christmas and 40 days before the Rest (Death) of the Virgin Mary (15th August) plus every Wednesday and (especially) Friday. Not as many people follow the strict rules of fasting privately but in public you avoid certain foods, such as dairy and meat, especially the week before Easter. In theory (Greek word) sex should also be avoided during these periods but few can resist. Don't worry tourists and travellers in general, as well as ill people, are exempt from this rule. Fasting has its origins in group dieting.

BAPTISM

Baptism in Greece is almost compulsory. It is unheard of for someone not to be baptised. It is done in a traditional way with the baby almost drowned in water. All relatives are present, as well as everyone who knows the parents, since it is a big insult to snub someone's baby's baptism. One of the biggest occasions in a Modern Greek's life, second only to marriage and death.

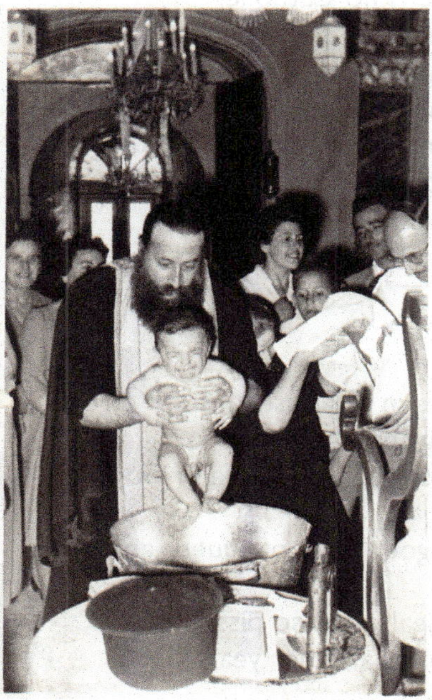

Greek baptism: an early introduction to public crying.

This photo is from the historic occasion of my own baptism (see next page for an in-depth commentary).

Three months after my birth, my parents baptised me as a Greek Orthodox Christian, without any consultation, nothing.
It was a cold Sunday morning when my parents led me to the church. There were many people there, I remember. Areti Leriopoulou was there with her husband Stylianos Leriopoulos, Konstantinos Kondoyiannakis and his wife Maria Kondoyiannaki. Even old sick Angelos Hadjigeorgiou came, as well as my uncle Spyridonas Giokarinis with his wife Eleni Giokarini and their kids Nikos and Dora. It was a brilliant turn-out, nine people, the whole village.
So, we arrive at the ceremony and to my amazement my parents hand me over to the old bearded priest who takes my little clothes off. I am flabbergasted! Naked, in front of everyone – I know. Everyone can see my member.
Ooh, it's left leaning like his dad's.
Bit small, hope it grows a bit.
At this stage I am very cold, embarrassed but I am not worried about paedophilic tendencies by the priest. He is no Catholic.
The old priest (stinking of cigarettes) mutters some words (it was all Greek to me) and when I start thinking that my ordeal is over he lifts me up in case anyone hadn't seen my member giving them all a good 'balls eye' view, removing any shred of remaining privacy. He then immerses me completely in a big font of cold water three times.
I am like, "Bgh gh bhg hg ..."
"Do you believe?"
"Bgh bgh bhg ..."
"Do you believe?"
Just like water-boarding.
My whole life flashes in front of my eyes in a nanosecond. All three months of it. Flashes of pooing, sleeping and boobs.
After the three immersions he declares, 'You are a slave of God now'.
Marvellous!
At the end of the ceremony everyone got a glass of liqueur and a biscuit. I got pneumonia.
At three months old this was a big ordeal. I was so pissed off with my parents I didn't speak to them for another year!

How To Raise Greek Children

1. Spend your whole life trying to find them a husband or wife and disapprove of every one they find on their own.
2. Spoil them rotten, but when they ask for something make them feel guilty for it.
3. Always compare them to other children (preferably those they don't like) when trying to make them do something.
4. Let them run around naked till they are 10 and thereafter buy them their clothes for as long as they will put up with. Once they start buying their own clothes always complain that they are too short, too tight, too low cut, too black, too cheap, not right for church or they give the wrong 'message' about your family.
5. Brag to your friends about how well behaved, beautiful and smart they are, but never tell them.
6. Always tell them they do not eat enough.
7. Be as strict as you can with your daughter(s) but let your son(s) get away with murder.
8. Embarrass them by getting drunk at name days, Easter, festivals, etc., and then drunk-dancing silly.
9. Assign a name to all their friends and use them at inappropriate occasions (i.e. the fat one, the ugly one, the dumb one, etc.).

10. Never let your daughter leave the house after 10 o'clock however old she is and tell her "good Greek girls don't behave that way" as many times as possible within a lifetime. Make her believe that Greek women never have sex.
11. Force them to go to church for as long as you can. Use blackmail if you have to, God would approve.
12. Buy them gold jewellery even when you know they only wear silver (because you like gold and it is more expensive).
13. Treat them like kids irrespective of how old they are.

GREEK WEDDINGS

What can I say? For an accurate description of every Greek wedding in Greece or abroad please see 'My Big Fat Greek Wedding'. This is not a film, it is a documentary. The only reason it did not win an Oscar is due to a Turkish conspiracy!

DEATH

Death is very central to Greek life, the result of Greek life to be more accurate (and any life for that matter). There is a strong tradition and numerous customs following the death of a person.

The underlying philosophy behind the aftermath of death customs has changed very little since ancient times. It is believed that although the soul has actually left the body of the dead person it is still around. Maybe it takes a while to say goodbye to everyone (Greeks are very social). The wandering soul needs to be taken care of and looked after before it finally moves on. The souls walk among the living if they are not comforted by light, incense and helped into paradise (all Greeks go to paradise according to the popular Greek belief) with prayers. The more people that pray and mourn the better. The more they pray and mourn the better. The louder they pray and mourn the more annoying and unsettling to other people.

Greek cemetery. Despite the legend Greek people also die.

Cremation of the body is not possible in Greece (even in 2014). Cremation is forbidden by the Greek Orthodox Church and people who specify they want to be cremated (in their will) are in danger of aphorism and being denied a religious burial. The theory goes that the body has been purified by the 'Holy Mysteria' and burial is really a deep sleep whilst you await the Second Coming.

To this day (yes, 2014), due to the lobbying of the Greek Church there are not any crematoriums in Greece. Therefore, dead Greek people who insist on cremation have to travel to Bulgaria (not an easy task when you're dead). Bulgarians have shown good business acumen and found a profitable niche market to make some money: death tourism.

Burial is justified on the grounds that when Jesus comes back to resurrect everyone, he won't be able to work with just ashes.

You can imagine Jesus saying, "You must be joking! Resurrect an urn of ashes? What am I, a miracle worker?"

The burial is carried out within 24 hours; in a hot climate it is good to get rid of a dead body quickly. A special ceremony is carried out every three months for the first year and on the second and then on the third year anniversary of the death. You can't forget, the local priest will remind you that you need to pay him. Death is an expensive business. Some cynics (Greek word) say that it us the money that the priests make after burial that make them so unwilling to allow cremation.

Sometime during the second year, once the coffin has settled in the ground, a small marble temple is built on the grave so it looks nice. At the top of each grave (which always looks to the east) there is a small shrine with a lamp and a picture of the dead at their best. For Greek people the need to look good goes beyond death. It is customary for the family of the dead person to visit the grave regularly to pay their respects. The family keeps the lamp lit and occasionally they light crumbs of charcoal and sprinkle them with grains of strong incense. Greek souls like that. They also like flowers and potted plants. The grave is decorated on public holidays and religious festivals so it does not feel left out.

After five to seven years, the grave gets de-constructed and the dead 'body' un-buried (exhumed). Exhumation can be an emotional and stomach-turning event. With any luck, there are only bones left in the coffin. Sometimes, if grave earthworms have had enough there are big pieces of flesh still on the bone. 'Indigestible' is a commonly used offensive word and refers to exactly this: a curse that you are not eaten fully by worms, but left for your relatives to see more of you than they want. Before being washed and dried the skull and bones are firstly passed around for hugs and kisses from the relatives. A show of love, that is. Then they are wrapped in a white cloth and placed in a small box which is placed in a special building within the graveyard to await the Second Coming (or at least until the relatives stop paying the 'maintenance' fees). This is all done so that when Jesus comes back he can easily stick all the boxes in the back of his van and take everyone up to heaven. Neat!

In the past, before modern medical advances in death determination, it was not unheard of to discover upon the exhumation that the dead had turned in their coffin, indicating that either the coffin was not comfortable for the corpse or that the person was not fully dead when buried. With burials having to be within 24 hours and people keen on their inheritance, old rich people did not sleep for too long at any one time.

The person who conducts the exhumation normally keeps any gold teeth the skull has left. He deserves it, don't you think?

> Personally, I would like to die like the ancient Greek philosopher Aeschylus. You know eagles love tortoise meat. The eagle flies down, grabs the tortoise, flies high up again and drops it smashing it to bits. Aeschylus was walking and philosophising in the countryside, when an flying eagle dropped a tortoise, on his head: Aeschylus was dead. What an interesting death! Everybody talks about it, even 2,500 years later!
> Or, you know when the police confiscate drugs they burn them (what a waste). I'd love to be on top of this furnace and take a deep breath of pure Iranian hashish and then fall in the fumes and fire. Two stones, one bird. A poetic death and two fingers up to the Greek Orthodox Church!

Public Celebrations and Holidays

Life is for celebrating and few do it better than the Greeks. Greek people work to live, they don't live to work. Greece has the highest number of national holidays (15), after Cyprus (19). There are of course more public celebrations at a local level. Every locality celebrates its local saint and its unification with Mama-Greece with a public holiday and at least half a day off work.

You may think Greece has enough holidays, but Greeks don't think so. There is strong campaigning and public support for two additional public holidays: July 4 (to celebrate winning the Euro in 2004) and August 13 (to celebrate starting the Olympics Games in 2004 on time). Everyone doubted the Olympics 2014 would ever happen due to budget restraints and the lack of urgency the Greek people showed. Despite this and some severe problems (the Greek government attributes these to secret Turkish agents) the Olympics were a great success. The only shame is that the various Olympic venues are not used today, with an annual cost of €60 million to just maintain them. Some people say the Government should have thought about possible future uses of the Olympic stadiums and facilities before they built them. These people are party poopers, the government replies.

Christmas

Christmas is not a huge thing in Greece. The Greek Church finds it premature to celebrate Jesus's birth as he only came good at Easter. The winter festivities are not a single event as Christmas (Christ is a Greek word: He who has the charisma), is the first part of a three-part celebration trilogy (Greek word).

The modest Christmas celebrations do not include the exchanging of presents nor a turkey based lunch but the main 'celebration' is a family meal, nonetheless.

The second part is New Year's Day, which is also St Vasillis's Day (a famous Greek Christian scholar). On New Year's Eve, playing cards throughout the night is very popular. If you win you start the New Year with some money, if not you can dream of luck in love, the theory goes. The third celebration is a two-in-one. The 'Fota' celebrates Christ's baptism (Greek word) and St John's day. On 'Fota' Day, the local priest 'baptises' the waters. Basically, during the special liturgy which is held by the sea, or a lake or a river or any other substantial volume of water, the priest pretends to 'drop' the cross in the water. Many, mostly young, men drop in the cold winter waters to 'find' it. It is a tough ancient custom, which led to the discovery of pneumonia (Greek word). The cross is then paraded all over the parish in exchange for donations from the faithful.

On Christmas Eve, New Year's Eve, and Fota Eve, kids go round houses singing the 'kalanda'. One or two minutes of songs of praise and well wishing in exchange for money. Like Halloween, but the opposite.

EASTER

Easter is by far the biggest religious celebration in the Greek calendar. One could argue it is only appropriate after everything Jesus went through to make Easter a memorable occasion. He almost killed himself for Christ's sake.

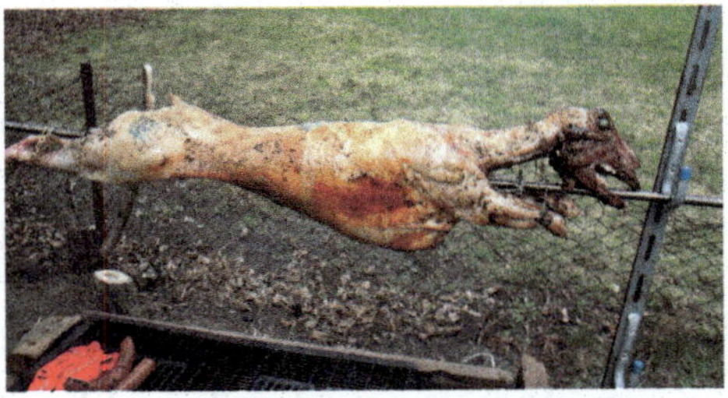

The traditional way to have the baby lamb (or the kid as in young goat) is on a spit. It smells great, it tastes great and it looks great!

Greek people celebrate Easter by eating meat (accompanied by more meat, ouzo, wine and more meat). The best meat available around Easter happens to be lamb, Jesus's favourite animal (some say it is ironic, some say it is what Jesus would want people to eat).

The preparation for Easter starts with a 40 day fast. No meat or dairy products, especially on Wednesdays and Fridays. Most Greeks nowadays do not follow the strict version, and observe fasting only during the week before Easter. Fasting does not include fish and seafood, which is considered more of a snack. When you fast time goes slower, hence, the week before Easter is called 'The Big Week'. On the Friday before Easter, ('Big Friday') for 48 hours Greek people do not even eat olive oil. The only time in the whole year that Greeks will not taste olive oil of any kind, for a whole 48 hours. A kind of torture for many Greeks!

The Resurrection of Christ happens on Sunday (at 00:00 to be exact) and some people say that the event is hastened by the priest somewhat as everyone is keen to start eating again. The announcement of the Resurrection is accompanied by huge noise from fireworks. The extremity of the celebrations leads to some deaths from the dangerous fireworks. This is a kind of social Darwinism, survival-of-the-one-who-can-make-safe-homemade-explosives.

After attending church on Saturday evening (very briefly) everyone heads home to start the eating. The customary dish is a sheep intestines soup, something hot and liquid to open up the stomach. The heavy meat eating can start seriously in the morning after a preparatory sleep.

The best starter for lamb is more lamb. It is called 'kokoretsi' (which means 'meat from a cockerel', inexplicably). It consists of the sheep's heart, lungs, kidney etc. wrapped in its intestines, grilled over a slow charcoal fire. Delicious! It has been a great delicacy for 2,000 years but the EU has decided that it is now bad and have banned it. The Greek people do not like this (like any other law) and the ban is flaunted on a huge scale. An alternative to a baby lamb is a young kid (not an actual kid but a young goat). The vegetarian option for Easter is lamb or goat bones.

The Rest of the Virgin Mary

The Rest of the Virgin Mary is celebrated on 15th August. It used to be a big religious festival but in modern times it has faded a little. The intense heat of August, the sea and all the tourists in bikinis make religious thinking tiresome. You simply can't think of God worshiping when you're in your swimming clothes.

The Day of the Holy Spirit

It falls in late June and is always on a Monday, which is great since a long weekend is guaranteed. The celebration was created so the Holy Spirit does not feel left out as every other religious entity has its own celebration day in the Greek Orthodox Church calendar.

25TH MARCH

The celebration that marks the start of the revolution against Ottoman rule on 25th March, 1821, which eventually led to the creation of the modern Greek state. It is celebrated by army and pupil parades in every major city. Girls wear skirts like the fighters of the 1821 revolution, but much, much shorter. Nice!

28TH OCTOBER

The celebration of the refusal by Greece to allow Italy to use Greek soil as 'a base for operations' in the Mediterranean sea on 28th October, 1940. In the subsequent war Greece kicked Italian ass. It is celebrated by army and pupil parades in every major city, too. Again, girls wear very short skirts (I am concerned that if global warming continues they may start parading in their underwear – not that many men would complain).

Greeks love a good parade: People of Samos parading in front of other people from Samos celebrating the Union of Samos with Mama-Greece, on 11 Nov 1912

Greek Cuisine

> Venture to any metro station or random street corner and you're bound to find a 'koulouri' stand selling rings of sesame coated bready delight to fend off hunger pangs and stuff into the mouths of screaming children. At 50 cents each they're a great way to get rid of spare change. The secret ingredient is the film of pollution covering each one. Mmmm....Tasty.

Greek people enjoy their food. Eating accompanied by drinking is the Greek national pastime of choice alongside coffee drinking, accompanied by smoking. It is not difficult to love Greek food; the cuisine is considered the best in the world (by all Greek people). It is quite easy to see why this could be true. Greece lies in the temperate climate with nutritional, colourful and varied ingredients (olive oil, vegetables, grains, honey, herbs, fish, poultry, goat, rabbit, and pork) and 5,000 years of trying different combinations of food and perfecting the recipes. Americans on the other hand....

In 330 BCE Archestratus wrote the first cookbook. He was the first ever food gourmet and he was Greek. This clearly indicates that cooking has always been of high significance in Greek society. Even the tall white chef's hat is owed to Greek history. In the middle ages, monks who prepared food in the Greek Orthodox monasteries wore tall white hats so that they could be distinguished from the normal monks who wore large black hats.

Greek mums use food to express their love. As a child you have to eat what you are offered. There is no way out as a true 'Greek Mum' will keep going on and on until you eat.

I visit my mum back in Greece regularly because I am Greek, I love her (and I want to check on the inheritance). Here's a typical dialogue (Greek word):
"Why don't you eat some cheese pies I made earlier? They are very good."
"I am not hungry mum, thanks."
"They are very nice, fresh. They will not be as good tomorrow. Eat some."
"I have just eaten, mum. I am not hungry, thanks."
"I made them today with my own hands. They are very good."
"I am not hungry, I tell you."
"I slaved in the oven for hours, and they are with the recipe of your dead grandmother. They are very good."
"Not just now mum, please."
"Why don't you have some cheese pies? Did I say they are very good?"
"I don't like them."
"Why don't you like them? Don't you love me? I made them for you."
"Ok, I'll have just one, then."
"You see I was right, you needed something to eat."

The older generation has a seemingly constant need to either eat or prepare food. This is a remnant from the Great Famine inflicted on Greece during the war to feed the occupying armies of Germany, Italy and Bulgaria. More than 50 years on, older Greeks have still not come to terms with the fact that we now have supermarkets and food available all year round. This mentality is 'inflicted' upon all Greek society. The victims are normally the young ones and the weak willed. You get stuffed with food on every occasion irrespective of your wishes. If you visit a Greek household, be prepared to eat. Refusal to eat what is offered to you is not taken lightly and it is considered bad manners.

Breakfast

The typical Greek breakfast is a Greek coffee and two or three cigarettes. This is the best way to finish off the digestion of the dinner from the night before (which was eaten relatively late by British standards). It is the only time that we do not eat much food. Breakfast is thought a degenerate, almost depraved habit for time wasters.

Greek people are not what you would call 'morning people' so spending 30-40 minutes eating seems a waste when you can spend it in bed and get up an hour later instead. The high nutritional value of the Greek coffee and the 'kick' of the nicotine is more than enough to provide the necessary energy until mid-morning. Then it is time to top up your energy levels by snacking on a 'healthy' filo-pastry type pie. These normally contain spinach and cheese (spanakopita), ham and cheese (zambonotyropita), bacon and cheese (baconotyropita) or just cheese and cheese (tiropita). For those with a sweet tooth it can be filled with cream (bougatsa). The snack is normally accompanied with the second coffee of the day.

LUNCH

Lunchtime is between 14:00-16:00 and lasts one to two hours (or more if you work as a civil servant). Lunch at home can be anything, even leftovers from yesterday's dinner. The only difference is the quantity of food rather than the actual dishes.

Normally it is a stew or a fry-up accompanied by white wine, ouzo or, during the summer, beer. It is customary that lunch is accompanied by a seasonal salad. Contrary to popular opinion abroad, we do not eat Greek salad all the time but a seasonal salad according to ...er... the season. During the winter, lettuce or cabbage-salad is especially refreshing.

Traditionally lunch is followed by a nap. Recently, scientists have discovered that a nap after lunch aids digestion reduces heart disease and leads to longevity. The science of the bleeding obvious. We have known this for thousands of years!

Foreigners used to mock our nap habit and took it as an indication of a low work rate. When they come and live in Greece for a while though, they soon realise that there is very little you can do during the hottest part of the day but to sleep it off and conserve your energy for later. They soon learn and happily adopt the habit.

Dinner

Dinnertime is traditionally between 21:00 to 24:00, and it's the main meal of the day. It normally consists of numerous dishes all brought at the same time. We do not have the concept of courses as we value interchanging tastes.

We consume large quantities of bread since ancient times. It is very nutritious and it is ideal to regulate the solid/liquid proportion of a meal; the key to a good meal and digestion.

Greek dishes and drinks

Greek salad

We call it 'choriatiki' (from the village); I don't know why, it normally comes from the kitchen. It consists of tomato, cucumber, green pepper, feta cheese, olives, olive oil, salt and pepper and oregano (optional). Some restaurants add lettuce which is a cheap way to bulk it up. When a Greek salad is accompanied by chips, it is the cheapest full lunch a tourist can have much to the despair of the restaurant owner.

Mousaka

Mousaka is a multi-layered dish made with sliced aubergines, sliced potatoes, lamb mince and cream. It's ironic (Greek word) that a dish which came to be associated with Greece, to represent Greek cuisine to a certain degree, is actually of Arabic origin (it came to Greece through Turkey, probably on foot). Needless to say the mousaka you eat in touristy restaurants has nothing to do with 'real' mousaka (nor any other dish for that matter).

My mum's stuffed vegetables. Before and after. Peppers, aubergines, tomatoes, vine leaves and courgette flowers!

> In restaurants in tourist areas mousaka has the extraordinary capacity to be kept fresh for four months.

STUFFED STUFF

The Greeks have liked stuffing things since ancient times. You name it, Greeks can stuff it. Peppers, aubergines, tomatoes, courgettes, courgette-flowers, chicken, turkey, goat's back, even things which at first glance do not seem stuff-able like vine leaves, cabbage leaves and onion layers. Greek stuffing is flavoursome, tasty and full of goodness. It is normally made with rice, dill and either mince or chopped offal (intestines, heart, liver, lungs and kidneys) of the animal to be stuffed (you could call it self-stuffing). Sounds nasty but it's very tasty and that's what Greek cuisine is all about: taste, health and leaving nothing to waste.

Fasolada

The real Greek national dish. Some could argue that fasolada is like baked beans, which is very wrong. Baked beans to 'fasolada' is what a McDonalds burger is to meat. No relationship. Greek 'fasolada' is made with beans, carrots, celery and sun-ripened tomato sauce: beautiful. Only one major side effect; beans produce gases which lead to flatulence. Symptoms start three hours after the meal and there is no antidote. 'Fasolada' is the perfect cure for coughing. After eating fasolada you're scared to cough.

For the first part of the 20th century a diet rich in 'fasolada' and other pulses (due to the scarcity of meat as a result of wars and poverty) led to the invention of the 'klaniola' (fart exhaust) which led to bedrooms with cleaner air. The 'klaniola' consisted of a hose one end of which was a bum receptor, the other end of which was put outside the bedroom. When you wanted (to be more accurate, you needed) to fart you place the bum receptor on your bum cheeks so the fart was exhausted outside the room. The 'fart exhaust' was considered necessary in upper class households, especially in the Ionian Islands. A Greek ingenuity that kept many marriages together.

Souvlaki and Gyros Pita

Souvlaki consists of small pieces of pork grilled on a skewer made of bamboo wood (bamboo does grow in Greece). It can be served on its own (kalamaki) or in a 'pita' (flat bread) with added tzatziki, tomato sauce, mustard, onions, salad, even chips. Souvlaki is ideal for lunch. It keeps you going until late evening when it's time for dinner. The popularity and 'fast-ness' of souvlaki has led to many modern versions: chicken souvlaki, swordfish souvlaki, even tofu souvlaki. Alternatively, the pita can be filled with 'gyros'. To make 'gyros', pieces of pork are placed on a tall vertical spit which turns in front of a heat source, usually an electric broiler. Admittedly, 'souvlaki pita' and 'gyros pita' both look a little like kebabs which has led some to believe that 'kebab' is a Greek dish, which is wrong. It does not even sound Greek. Kebab is Turkish, a hard sounding, silly word. Souvlaki or 'gyros' are normally made from pork, which makes them very anti-Taliban, very anti-terrorist and very anti-Turkish.

The concept of souvlaki is very Greek though. We have been eating souvlaki and gyros since ancient times. You can find the original recipe in some of the most famous ancient Greek theatre plays: 'Acharnians', 'Birds and Wasps' by Aristophanes, 'Politics' by Aristotle and 'Hellenica' by Xenophon.

Tzatziki

A thick white side dish, which can also be used as a sauce. It is made with proper thick Greek yoghurt, grated cucumber, crushed garlic and a tiny bit of salt, pepper, olive oil and vinegar. The result looks very much like the sperm of someone who hasn't had sex for a while (with the cucumber resembling little sperms swimming around) but tastes great. Beware: even moderate consumption of tzatziki tends to keep the members of the opposite sex far away. Not sure you will eat it again after the above metaphor, anyway!

Feta

The white cheese that came to symbolise Greece. After years of fighting with the European Union, feta is now officially a product with controlled origin status. Denmark can no longer produce tasteless white cheese called feta. Feta is best served sliced and sprinkled with olive oil, pepper and oregano.

There are other great Greek cheeses. 'Kefalotyri' (translates to 'head cheese') is great for grating or accompanying ouzo or fried. It is similar to 'kefalograviera' (translates to 'head of graviera') and they are both made from a mixture of sheep and goat's milk. They are yellow to white and salty. Try them.

Octopussy

A very tasty delicacy and the best accompaniment to ouzo. It is normally grilled, as when you try to boil it can take hours – it keeps switching the gas off with its long tentacles. The Turkish do not eat octopus as they consider it a creature of the devil. They will not even touch it because it is slimy.

KALAMARIA

Also known as 'kalamares' by tourists that cannot pronounce Greek words well. It is squid in English. It is best prepared tossed in flour, fried and served with lemon.

'Kalamaria' are small round animals that live at the bottom of the sea.

OLIVES AND OLIVE OIL

Olives and olive oil have been closely associated with Greece since ancient times. The wealth of ancient Greece was largely due to the production and distribution of olives and olive oil throughout the Mediterranean basin. Always choose non-pitted olives, they are much more tasty, the way they should be. Green, black, small, big, olives in brine or not in brine they are all good and very nutritious. Olives and virgin olive oil constitute a big part of the modern healthy Greek diet and the secret to our longevity. The most famous are the 'Kalamata' olives (Kalamata is a Greek town). Large, tasty with a hint of vinegar.

Greek olives: the result of olive oil compression. Very tasty.

Bread

Bread accompanies every Greek meal. How people in other countries are able to eat without bread remains a mystery to Greek people. With bread around there is always a possible meal. Grilled bread with some olive oil, salt, pepper and oregano is a traditional healthy snack (or an expensive starter in a restaurant). Add some cheese and tomato and you know where the Italians got the idea (Greek word) for the pizza, the basis for the whole Italian cuisine.

Ouzo

The throat-burning, stomach-churning, head-shuddering ouzo is a magical drink. It is transparent like water but when you add water to it it becomes white. Just like that. Magic! It is twice distilled from grape skins with added aniseed, liquorice, coriander, angelica root, mint, wintergreen, fennel, hazelnut and cinnamon depending on the area. It is good for indigestion, breastfeeding, flatulence and bad breath, diarrhoea, libido and toothache. It is also great for a piss up. Deeply associated with Greek culture despite being first brewed in 1853.

RETSINA

A truly Greek wine. Retsina is produced by putting blocks of pine resin in the grape juice before it's made into wine. What a great idea! It gives it a refreshing taste, makes it last longer and fortifies the liver. It is a perfect accompaniment to the Greek cuisine and is drunk in small glasses, not the usual wine glasses. It's an informal drink, the drink of the Greek working classes - like cider in UK, but better.

GREEK COFFEE

A favourite with the older generation and modern hippies (or poor people). A great accompaniment to smoking. A Greek coffee is normally enough for two cigarettes. Small, dark brown and strong like a Greek child in the middle of the summer. Greeks used to be very particular about their coffee; there are 15 types of Greek coffee, depending on the combination of coffee quantity, amount of sugar and appearance. Never add milk to Greek coffee, it is considered blasphemy (Greek word) or a sign of illness.

You will find it in the whole Eastern Mediterranean basin called Turkish coffee, Lebanese coffee etc. It is actually imported from Brazil and made from the same beans as all types of coffee around the world from the fashionable espresso to the lowly Greek coffee.

We Greeks used to call Greek coffee Turkish coffee until Turkey invaded Cyprus in 1974. After the invasion it seemed un-patriotic to order a Turkish coffee so we renamed the humble beverage Greek coffee. You invade Northern Cyprus and rename it the Turkish Republic of N. Cyprus? We change the name of your coffee, see how you like it. An eye for an eye, a tooth for a tooth, tit for tat.

The Greek coffee is a metaphor (Greek word) for life itself. The coffee represents the bitterness that we have suffered in life. Sugar symbolises the sweet moments we enjoy in life and the froth on top...well it's just froth.

FRAPPE

The coffee of the Modern Greek. Frappe is one of the major Greek inventions as it assists the human body to cool down whereas at the same time enhancing his caffeine levels. It is the perfect accompaniment to a smoking session. It can accompany five cigarettes, but some people will happily smoke seven cigarettes with each frappe. The current record is 13 cigarettes with a single frappe. It is held by Stavros Troumbas, a medical student.

How to make frappe coffee:

1. Locate your nearest coffee shop.
2. Have ready with you an empty water bottle. If you don't, buy a water bottle and tip its contents down a drain.
3. Through elaborate sign language, acquire one glass, a few sachets of sugar, a few sachets of coffee, a straw, a glass of ice water and a little milk (optional).
4. Pour sugar, coffee and a little water into the empty water bottle you have prepared.
5. Shake bottle vigorously until you have a creamy light brown concoction.
6. Pour mixture into empty glass.
7. Top up with ice water, a little milk and a straw.
8. Enjoy!
9. Compliment your invention loudly so that the Spanish get an idea of what they're missing.

Frappe is a very versatile coffee, you can have it with ice cream in it (and pay three times the price), Baileys (for an extra kick) or most commonly milk. A great Greek invention for the world!

The Invention of Frappe

Frappe was invented by Dimitrios Vakendios, an employee of the Greek distributor of Nestle in 1957. During the International Exhibition at Thessalonica, his boss Ioannis Dritsas was presenting a new chocolate drink for kids, which you could make instantly by mixing it with milk in a shaker. Dimitrios wanted to have a coffee but could not find any hot water, so he 'shook' some coffee, water and sugar and the first frappe was a reality.

Frappe: Half froth, half coffee, full price.

Whisky

A relative newcomer to the Greek diet (Greek word). It was soon adopted as a key characteristic (Greek word) of the Modern Greek. For some time in the 1980s, the fight was undecided between whisky and vodka. West and East fought for the favour of the Greeks' throats but Greeks have chosen firmly and decided in favour of the West. Greeks were the biggest drinkers of whisky in the world per capita (four and a half bottles per person – babies included). A Greek actually drank more whiskey than a Scot! Strange but true. Following the crisis many Greeks have returned to more traditional drinks like wine and beer (money changes taste, it seems).

Tea

Tea drinking is not recommended while in Greece; it looks weird and is considered strange. Greece never had an empire which included tea producing countries; hence tea drinking is not as common there. Greek people drink tea when they have an upset stomach (Greek word) and it is normally served with a piece of lemon. If you ask for tea with milk, don't be surprised if people gather around you trying to take your temperature and offering you a lift to the nearest hospital; tea with milk indicates severe illness, and it is normally accompanied with an aspirin. Treat your holiday as a period (Greek word) of tea detoxification and save everyone the trouble.

Greek Institutions

Close Family and 'Spiti' (Family Home)

Family is the most important institution within the Greek society. It stands above all else, even Mama-Greece itself. If you want anything you go to your family first. The rest of the family (especially your mum) will effectively micromanage most of your life from birth to death and beyond. The only thing you do outside your family is marriage (apart from Samothrace, a northern Greek island, it's our Norfolk).

Greek men and women are expected to stay in their family homes ('spiti') until they get married. It is not common for the children to move out of the parental home before marriage (it is not uncommon to stay next to the parents after the marriage, either). Single parents and people living on their own are not common. Greeks like company, and the society (like most of the Mediterranean societies) is very traditional.

Advantages of staying at home with your parents until marriage:

- You get the best cook (your mum) to cook two free meals a day for you (meals you generally choose)
- You have your clothes washed and ironed
- There are no bills to pay (no Greek parent would accept money from their kids)

Disadvantages of staying at home with your parents till marriage:

- Lack of privacy (not a Greek thing anyway).
- Adverse effect on your sex life (and that of your parents)

Greek men, especially in the last 20 years or so have some kind of choice whether to move out or not, but not the 'good' girls. A Greek girl who moves out of her parental home to live on her own acquires a status slightly better than a trainee prostitute by the all too critical Greek society, especially outside Athens.

Due to 'society values' and brainwashing as a child, being Greek you feel the 'need' to have a good relationship with your parents. Unfortunately, your parent's opinion matters to you more than you would like it to. I still do things and eat food I don't like just because my mum insists I do – and I am 36. The few people that did use to live on their own moved back with their parents due to the economic crisis.

Cohabiting or sharing is not common – which makes the cost of moving out even higher. Living together with people who are not blood relatives or to whom you are not married, is thought to be for poor people and gypsies. If a guy lives with another guy it is thought to be very suspicious (i.e. gay). If two girls live together no worries, they are certainly lesbians. If single people live in a mixed household they are having orgies every night, the small minded thinking goes.

I come from a very progressive family and moved out shortly after my 30th birthday (two years later to be exact) so I could spend some time alone with my girlfriend. My move gave my parents the opportunity to move out of the family home themselves – without me in the house there was no reason to stay with my grandparents.
My parents moved out about a month after I moved out so they could come and stay …next to me. Therefore, I had a word with them:
"Mum, dad, I love you lots but I am 36 now and I want to try to live completely on my own away from you."
An hour later when they regained consciousness, I tried to argue that I needed to learn to be self-sufficient, to wash and iron my own clothes and that I could survive without my mum's cooking, but they were having none of it.
"Is there anywhere I can go that you will not follow me?"
"Only if you move away from Greece, to a cold country where people talk strange and eat weird stuff."
So, I moved to Britain!

Greek Women

Despite appearances, the Greek society is essentially matriarchal; the macho Greek male has a mostly decorative role. It's like the male lion, looking all pretty and hairy but not doing much apart from being loud and proud of himself. It is normally the wife that has the financial control and dictates the social calendar of the couple.

With marriage, the Modern Greek Man is passed over from his mum (the woman who dominates the first 30-35 years of his life) to his wife (who dominates the rest of his life, at least until the divorce). From woman to woman, like a product with instructions:

"Take good care of him, feed him well. He loves lamb. And make sure he has at least one shower a week."

Greek women do not normally allow Greek men to be involved in food preparation or dish washing, simply because Greek men are not any good at it.

Typical dialogue between me (in London) and my mum (in Samos):

"Hello Mum."
"Hello my son, where have you been?"
"What do you mean 'where have I been'? We only spoke two days ago."
"Do you know what can happen in two days? It only takes a second for something bad thing to happen."
"So, shall I call you every second?"
"Why not? ... Niki's son went out for a coffee, he slipped on the pavement and he broke his leg."
"So shall I never go out for a coffee, mum. Please!"
"Do you wear a beanie?"
"Inside the house? Are you crazy, Mum?"
"Why? Do you wear a beanie outside the house?"
"Nobody wears a beanie!"

"I don't care what the others do. I only care for my child. You should wear a beanie to cover your ears. If your ears are exposed you'll catch a cold!"

"It's not cold, Mum!"

"Every time you tell me 'it is not cold'. But when you catch a cold it is me who will be sick with worry. I will die and I will be worried about you. I will die from worry. You are a grown man now, but you don't think properly."

"I know what I am doing mum."

"You don't know. You are only a little child!"

"So what am I? A grown man or a little child?"

"Do you wear the woollen gloves I made you? Cold hands lead to a cold!"

"I am wearing them."

"You are not. You are lying to me to get rid of me. Next thing you will be walking with your bare feet on the floor and you will catch a cold. If your feet are cold, you will catch a cold."

"I am not in Siberia, mum. I am in London."

"Maria, Giorgos's wife told me that her son Giannis told her that is very cold in London."

A traditional society Greece may be, but divorce is increasingly common. Rhodes is the divorce capital of Greece. 30% of all marriages end in divorce. Probably due to the temptation posed by the high quality of tourist totty that arrives in the island every summer.

"And I am telling you that it is not cold in London."
"Why should I believe you and not Giannis?"
"Because Giannis does not live in London. And he is 12 years old!"
"Do you wear your scarf at least? You need to cover your throat to avoid a cold. If your throat is cold you will catch a cold."
"Yes mum. It is 22 degrees outside and Manos the crazy Greek will go out with a beanie, gloves and scarf. Why not with thermal underwear, long johns and a hot water bottle under each arm."
"I will send you feta cheese in a parcel. You like feta cheese."
"No mum. I don't particularly like feta cheese. They sell feta cheese here, too"
"What are you talking about? The feta cheese in Britain is not the same. You can give some to your boss; maybe he will give you a pay rise. Did you have a shower this week?"
"What are you talking about? If I have a shower, I may get a cold!"
"Shall I send you some thermal underwear? You need to change your underwear every day. If something happens and you go to hospital you need to have clean underwear all the time!"
"Mum, I am losing signal."
"Is your mobile charged?"
"Yes it is. I am charged too…"
"You need to have it charged all the time. If anything happens to you, call me for advice immediately. Stavros, Marigoula's son…"
"Mercy mum. I can't take any more advice"
"I need to give you advice, so you know what to do. That's what mums are for. If I don't give you advice, who will? The British? They are foreigners."

"But you do this all the time mum. Every time we speak! Why are you doing this to me?"
"You only have one mum!"
"That's lucky. Imagine if I had two!"

'Filotimo'

The closest English word to the Greek word 'filotimo' is 'reciprocation', but it does not do it justice. It's a very Greek thing. Someone who has 'filotimo' is a 'friend of honour'. 'Filotimo' is non-calculating, and it is done neither in reciprocation nor in anticipation of a favour in return. It's an internal 'force' that 'makes' you want to reciprocate to someone who's done you good, that makes you want to look after someone less fortunate than you. It's your inner Greek Buddha, if you like. It's what makes you offer the best you have to a visitor (which explains the eagerness of Greeks to help tourists).

Birthdays and Name-days

In Greece, birthdays are not big occasions. Greek people do not see what there is to celebrate. Getting older is not exactly a cause for a party. The occasion is normally marked with a few drinks with your mates, drinks you buy. Let me make it absolutely clear: it is YOUR celebration, it's YOUR birthday, YOU buy people drinks. It is like what the British do, but the exact opposite.

What is a big celebration for a Greek person is his or her name day. When it comes to names the custom is for the first boy to take the name of his paternal grandfather and any girls the name of their grandmothers, however old-fashioned the name sounds. Greek people don't name their kids according to their favourite soft drink, or the place they conceived or random fruits so you will not find any Greek people called 'Sprite', 'Brooklyn', or 'Peaches'. On the other hand you end up with names such as 'Charalambos', 'Tsampbikos' and 'Evangelos'. Exactly. They don't sound good in Greek, either. The solution around the old fashioned sounding names is the use of nicknames. Charalambos becomes 'Babis', Tsambikos becomes 'Tsamp' and 'Evangelos' becomes 'Vagelis' and Emmanouil becomes Manolis, Makis or Manos.

One's name day is the feast day of the saint whose moniker it shares. If someone has an uncommon or ancient Greek name, which is not covered by the more than 10,000 saints of the Orthodox Church, no problem. There is an All Saints Day, so everyone can have a name day. Genius!

The Catholic Church has about 10,000 saints (78 of them ex-Popes), whereas the poor Anglican Church has only one, King Charles I of England.

The name day is a big event, it is a proper celebration. The smallest celebration one does is a 'dinner party' at home with family and guests bringing a gift, normally a houseplant, flowers or a box of pasties. The normal celebration is a night out at 'bouzoukia'. As there are many people with the same name in any town, city or village usually a friendly competition will ensue for the best dance and to see who's the biggest spender (or at least that was the case before the economy went down the drain).

If it is your name day and you don't want to have a celebration you would normally put it in the local newspaper (or Facebook, these days) and tell everyone you know. Otherwise you will end up having people around your house anyway. Greeks do not need an invitation to come around, not on your name day (or any day for that matter).

Malaka

'Malaka' is the most famous Greek word and it is used with very high frequency especially by the younger Greeks who use it every two to three other words. It is the first word Greek babies say, legend has it. It can be used for a man or a woman, and it is the only word in the Greek language that is used in the same form for a man or woman. It can be used instead of 'good morning', 'good afternoon' 'friend', somebody's name etc. It literally means 'he who chronically masturbates' or simply 'wanker'. It can also mean 'ill', 'anti-social', 'tosser' anything you want really; it's all in the tone and the occasion.

Generally, and between friends it is a term of endearment. There is something special about the first time you call someone 'malaka'. You break a social barrier; you become closer to him or her as a person. Since everyone does masturbate (at least all men) admitting to it brings you closer, you realise you are facing the same sexual problems and that neither of you is perfect.

It is one thing to be called 'malaka' by a fellow Greek and a different thing altogether to be called 'malaka' by a 'non-Greek'. Most Greeks will grin and bear it, but that does not mean they like it when a 'non-Greek' uses the word. When you call a Greek person 'malaka' you'll notice he starts using the word 'bastard' quite frequently and his tone changes.

'Malaka' should not be confused with the similarly sounding 'makaka' which means 'he who chronically masturbates other people'. 'Makaka' is not a term of endearment, its one thing to unload yourself from time to time and it's another thing to make a living out of it.

BASTARD

In Greece, we take things literally and the above word is one of the most severe insults to a Greek as it means you don't know who your father is. It's a certain way to start a fight, and believe me

Greeks don't start a fight easily (we prefer to make love or masturbate).

> HEALTH WARNING: Addressing a Greek person with the word 'bastard' can seriously damage your health. Greek people take the circumstances of their conception very seriously. You have been warned!

SWEARING

Greek people frequently mix swear words into their normal everyday talk (apart from bastard). The more at ease they feel with the people they are conversing with the more and the stronger the swear words. Common swear words and phrases include 'pousti' (passive homosexual), 'aderfi' (passive homosexual), 'gamo to Theo mou/Dia mou' (f*** my God/Zeus), 'gamo ton Christo mou' (f*** my Christ), 'gamo tin Panagia mou' (f*** my Virgin Mary), 'gamo ton stavro mou' (f*** my Holy Cross), 'kolopaido' (a***-boy), 'keratas' (horn-bearing man, meaning cuckold). Unsurprisingly, they all relate to sexual acts.

Below are some popular Greek phrases that are not so rude, translated to English and their meaning. Use them in their English translation to amuse and gain respect. You will not find these in any Greek-English dictionary.

Are you working me?	Do you think I am stupid?
He/she farted me.	He/she ignored me.
He/she returned me the entrails	I dislike him/her

I saw the Christ soldier	I got scared.
I don't know Christ	I know nothing.
I took my three (as in two balls and one penis)	I lost.
Aaah! Of the gay	He is lucky!
Shit and from shit	Shit.
Shit high and gaze	Stay out of it.
They became robes - robes unbuttoned	They had a good time.
We confused our thighs	We got confused.
Who's banister**	It's complicated.
You owe me your horns	You owe me a lot.
You ate my ears	Shut up.

There is no need to be intimidated by all the swearing, the loudness and the hand gestures that normally accompany Greeks talking. It is all for show, enjoy it.

'Peripτero' (Pavement Kiosk)

One of the most quintessentially Greek institutions. They can provide you with all the essentials (cigarettes, alcoholic drinks, key rings, toilet paper etc.) almost any time of day or night. In fact, if you want to know when the nightlife stops in a town all you have to do is to ask what time the central 'periptero' shuts (if ever).

Licences for a 'periptero' are much sought after as they are limited. These licences used to be awarded to injured war veterans of the various wars, but as we have hardly been at war lately the Government now awards them to any severely disabled person with connections to the local council, who in turn 'rents' the place for a handsome fee. Running a modern kiosk is hard work, but very lucrative as newspapers and cigarettes are essential for the lifestyle of the Modern Greek. Kiosks are supposed to be two to three square metres but some of them manage to extend to five or six square metres. They belong to owners with good connections. A great fortune awaits the entrepreneur who will transplant this business idea to another country.

SMOKING

For most Greeks smoking is a human right and part of the Greek identity. To be a non-smoker is to be non-Greek. Actually, recent studies have confirmed that Greek people are genetically engineered to smoke.

Smoking accompanies Greek breakfast, Greek coffee, frappe, lunch, dinner, drinking and every waking moment. In fact, many older Greeks get up in the middle of the night to have a couple of sneaky fags to top up the all-important nicotine level. In Greece, smoking is a serious activity; no baby packs of 10 cigarettes.

A number of Governments has tried to impose restrictions on where and when smoking is permitted, but time after time it has failed. Greeks have been defying smoking bans since 1856, when King Otto and Queen Amalia prohibited smoking inside state buildings. In the modern era, there was another attempt in 2009 when the Greek Parliament (under pressure from the EU) voted to ban smoking in enclosed places. Following protests and demonstrations, the Government accepted some 96 exceptions to the law, which basically made the ban unworkable. Perhaps more importantly they took away any punishment for those who actually broke the law. There were further attempts in 2010 and 2011, and 2013. They all failed because Greeks treasure their freedom to smoke.

LAW OBEDIENCE

Greek people value their freedom above all. This includes freedom from the law. Apart from the smoking ban, laws regularly flouted include the one about not building a house without permission, the one about not driving when clearly drunk, not parking where it is not permitted, paying taxes on your income and so many others. In fact, if you want something done in Greece it is best to make a law against it. The story about the introduction of potatoes to Greece demonstrates that.

King Otto (in the 1830s) knew that the Greeks would reject out of hand any suggestion that they plant or eat potatoes. As such, he carefully let slip that a precious cargo had arrived in Piraeus (the port city of Athens) whose contents were exclusively for the Royal family and would punish anyone caught stealing potatoes. Some Greeks boarded the loosely-guarded ship at night and hijacked the precious cargo for themselves. Soon afterwards, the potato appeared frequently on Greek menus.

Hospitals

Apart from making a law against it, the other way to have something done in Greece is bribery. Nowhere is this truer than the health service. If you get ill and you want to get well soon, prepare to hand over some money. Although officially illegal for a few years now doctors (and nurses) expect a small envelope with some cash to move your case forward. It is a similar system to the private health service in the U.K. but more direct!

The Evil Eye

If things are not going well for you, it may be because you are under the spell of the 'evil eye', known as 'mati'. The 'eye' is known to have been a fixture in Greece dating back to at least the 6th century BCE, when it commonly appeared on drinking vessels. The evil eye is cast away through the process of 'xematiasma' whereby the 'healer' silently recites a secret prayer passed over from an older relative of the opposite sex, usually a grandparent. Such prayers are revealed only under specific circumstances, for according to superstition those who reveal them indiscriminately lose their ability to cast off the evil eye.

How do you know whether you are under the spell of the 'evil eye':

1. You yawn profusely.
2. Your libido is non-existent (your appetite for sex with your usual partner does not count).
3. Everything that can go wrong, does.

The evil eye has many fans/believers across the Balkans and the Middle East.

All of Greece is thought to be afflicted by the 'evil eye' in recent years.

GREEK LIFE RHYTHM

(Greek word)

When in Greece do as the Greeks. Most foreigners who live in Greece, and some tourists in their first week, never get it and try to live to an 'industrialised' timetable. The 'slave-timetable' as it is called in Greece.

Hours (Greek word) are not as relevant in Greece. Greek people are flexible and they don't like time restraints. There is morning, noon, afternoon, evening and dinnertime.

Greek Words In The English Language

Greek people are very proud of the contribution the Greek language has made to other languages, and especially of the number of Greek words in the English language, all 56,186 of them, and they will not lose a chance to remind you when you use an English word of Greek origin.

What does it mean if a word is Greek, English or French? In most cases it means that the people (or at least one person) identified something and named it. Take for example 'garage' a French word. It is so because it was a French guy that first thought to himself:, 'We need a name for the 'room-where-we-keep-the-car'. Let's call it 'garage'.'

Here are a few Greek words and their meanings:

Philosophy Talking about thinking.

Clitoris From the Greek word 'kleidi' meaning key. The key to a woman's pleasure.

Aeroplane A plane full of air.

O.K.	Short for 'Ola Kala' meaning everything is good. The use of this word originates from when custom officers of Greek-origin at US customs used to inspect parcels and mark the good ones with OK (Ola Kala).
Politics	'Poli' means city, and tics are blood sucking insects.
Architect	'Archi' is the first syllable of the Greek word archidi (bollocks or balls). 'Tect' means 'to draw a line'. Therefore 'architect' is the guy who does not have the balls to be an engineer but he is not gay enough to be a graphic designer.
Monarch	'Mon' means one, and 'arch' means bollocks, balls. Therefore 'monarch' is the king with one ball. When the Athenians discovered that their king had one ball (during an orgy), they said bollocks to him and they invented democracy.
Orgasm	A lot of things going on at the same time.
Homophones	Words that sound similar (what did you think?)

Greeks have borrowed two English words, both very useful.

Until recently some one would say, "Hey, Stavros! Do you want to take our wives and kids, prepare some food, drinks, and drive to the countryside, find a tree, put a cloth down and eat until we cannot eat any more, look at the grass, take pictures of how happy we are, and how healthy we look in nature?"

Now it's much simpler: "Hey Stavros, shall we have a '**picnic**'?"

Relax is the other English word Greek people have started using recently, mostly associated with watching TV or sleeping.

Greek Phrases In The English Language

Below some of the most popular Greek phases (Greek word) in the English language and their meaning.

When somebody '**doesn't give a jot**' they imply that they don't care at all about something. The origins of that phrase are from ancient Greece. The original phrase was 'I don't give one iota', 'iota' being the smallest letter in the Greek alphabet.

When someone is '**lily livered**' there are thought to be a coward. Ancient Greeks believed that the liver of a cowardly person was pale and lily-coloured. This was because if the liver of a sacrificed animal on the eve of a battle was pale and lily coloured it was thought to be a bad omen as opposed to a red and full of blood one which was a good omen.

An adaptation of 'meli-muthos' which means 'honey speak' is '**mealy mouthed**' meaning a person who is unwilling to speak plainly.

'**Spondulics**' is slang for money and it is derived from Ancient Greece. It has two possible and potentially complementary explanations. One possible origin is the word 'spondulikos' (a type of seashell) which was used as money for a short time and the other one is 'spondylos' (meaning spine) as a stack of coins resembles a spine. John Mitchell in his book 'A Manual of the Art of Prose Composition' in 1867 supports the second version.

The origin of '**to kill the goose that lays the golden egg**' can be found in one of Aesop's fables. The moral of the fable is to advise patience and caution against greed. By the way, Aesop was born in Samos (like me) and spent much of his life away from Samos (like me) as a slave (unlike me).

The phrase '**sour grapes**' also originates from one of Aesop's fables. It is used to describe someone who is sulking due to not having something he wants.

'**Achilles' Heel**' is the weakness in someone or something otherwise very powerful. Thetis (Achilles's mother) dipped him in Styga (the holy river), when he was a baby in order to make him impenetrable. But she held him from his heel which remained out of the water, so was his only vulnerable spot. Paris (whose brother Achilles killed) learned of this (by a meddling God) and killed him with an arrow shot straight at his heel during the Trojan War. More details of this story are to be found in Illiad or the film 'Troy' with a blond Brad Pitt as Achilles.

To keep something '**at bay**' is to fend off a danger or illness. Ancient Greeks (and later Romans) would seek shelter under a bay tree during a storm as they had noticed that bay trees never seemed to be struck by lightning. Warriors often took to wearing bay leaves as protection against the enemy and thunderstorms. There is no evidence it worked. During the Great Plague of London in 1665 the people of London did the same in the hope they would avoid the plague (i.e. keep it at bay). There is no evidence that worked either.

When someone is described as a '**real brick**' they are thought to be reliable and dependable. It originates from Lycurgus, a king of Sparta who refused to build defensive walls around Sparta. When asked why he replied that 'every one of his soldiers was a brick'. Interestingly, 'a real brick' in modern Greece means someone very stupid.

'**Eat your heart out**' is a good humoured taunt. It goes back to Pythagoras (he was also born in Samos, like me) who 2,500 years ago advised 'Do not eat your heart' meaning 'don't waste your life worrying about something'.

Something is in the '**lap of the gods**' when the outcome is unclear and cannot be influenced in any way. It originates from Homer's Iliad where Automedon declared 'these things lie in the knees of the Gods' regarding the battle after Patroclos's death.

SERVICE

You can expect great service in Greece as Greek people do not see the provision of service as a lowly job. In turn a good tip is expected of five to ten percent of the value of the purchased products.

> The first time I went to a pub in the UK I sat on a table; I waited for a while, then I waited some more, nothing. Nobody came to greet me and thank me for coming. I had chosen that establishment out of a dozen I had seen on the way there, but no gratitude for my choice. I had to even go myself and get a drink. I had to queue for a grumpy Australian youth to serve me when he could be bothered. Then the ultimate disrespect and expression of distrust: money up front. Like I was some kind of cheapskate and would go without paying (it had occurred to me, though). I gave no tip.

In Greece you can expect your car to be filled with petrol instead of you getting out of the car. Stay in the car, window down

"Fill it up please."

Give the money, off you go! In the UK you have to get outside the car fill it up yourself and then go and pay. What next? Will we be forced to refine the crude oil?

No tip is expected at petrol stations.

Bug Eye Sunglasses (Irrespective of the Sunlight Intensity)

To the Modern Greek (man and woman), these are as much a part of being human. Wear them and enjoy the advantages of looking super cool while gazing at any part of anyone's anatomy undiscovered.

Taxis

Taxis (Greek word, from the word taxi-di which means trip) are very cheap in Greece. They look like normal cars but they are of a specific colour depending on the town and they are still driven by Greeks rather than first or second-generation immigrants. Taxis are a 'closed' (i.e. a protected) profession in Greece so the driver is the owner of the car. Beware of any 'impolite' comments about the car. Taxi drivers double up as psychotherapists (Greek word), confession listeners, psychologists (Greek word), doctors and all round fixers. If they don't know something, they usually know someone people who does. Use them.

It is advisable to sit in the front seat, declaring informality and friendliness (it's also a good way to check they don't fiddle with the meter).

Everyone Is Against Us Because Greek People Are So Great

Greeks are naturally suspicious of everything and see conspiracy against them everywhere.

Although Greek people are not known for their ability to laugh at themselves they tell a story about their tendency to come up with and believe in conspiracy theories. They relate how God decided that he would give every nation as a gift a special national characteristic. On the appointed day, representatives of the nations of the world entered the divine presence and were handed their gifts. The Americans received optimism, the French elegance, the British stoicism, the Russians courage, the Iranians cunning; and so on the stereotypical saying goes.

The Greek delegation was delayed and arrived late just as the other nations were leaving. God apologised and explained to them that he was sorry but he had already given away the most desirable characteristics and there were none left. The Greeks were enraged and protested furiously, shouting "so you too, God, have joined the plot against us as we always expected you would. Go on, tell us who is paying you and why do you conspire against us?" Angered in turn, God said: "Very well, you Greeks will have a gift in keeping with your accusations. In future, it will be part of your national character to always believe in conspiracy to explain everything that happens to you."

According to a recent survey published in Greek newspapers, one in three Greeks believes that they are being sprayed with chemical or biological agents from a high altitude. A right-wing party led by Panos Kammenos (his surname means 'burned') put a question to the Greek parliament demanding that 'chemtrails' stop!

The poll also revealed that women of ages 18-24, are most worried most about the chemtrails. In Greece there is an organization supporting the belief that chemtrails are genocide and a crime against humanity.

'They are spraying us so we become mad'

The mother of all Greek conspiracy theories is that the Big Powers conspire to destroy Greece because they are jealous of the Greek people (since they are great and marvellous). When you ask for evidence the following quote is recited (most Greek people know it by heart): 'The Greek people are anarchic and difficult to tame.

For this reason we must strike deep into their cultural roots: Perhaps then we can force them to conform. I mean, of course, to strike at their language, their religion, their cultural and historical reserves, so that we can neutralize their ability to develop, to distinguish themselves, or to prevail; thereby removing them as an obstacle to our strategically vital plans in the Balkans, the Mediterranean, and the Middle East' This quote was reported in the popular Greek magazine, Oikonomikos Tachydromos on 14

August 1997. Allegedly it was by Henry Kissinger, while addressing a group of Washington, D.C. businessmen in September 1974. Henry Kissinger has of course denied saying the above or being in Washington at that time. But then again he would wouldn't he?

Needless to say the overwhelming majority of Greek people (72% according to a recent survey) firmly believe that the economic crisis was caused by the EU and the major European Governments (backed up by Big Capital) in order for them to get hold of the Greek oil and gas. There are no proven deposits of oil or gas in Greece but facts are secondary to a good conspiracy theory.

When in Greece, you will undoubtingly see a lot of rubbish by the roadsides. This may lead you to believe that Greek people have little respect for the law, the environment or their fellow Greek people. This may be true but it is also wrong.
Throwing rubbish by the roadside is considered (especially by the people who throw the rubbish) as the best way for future generations to discover art and crafts from our era, the way we dig up marbles and statues from ancient times.

Driving

Greek drivers are the best in the world. They need to be in order to cope with the bad roads and the other Greek drivers. The most important thing to know is that following normal driving rules is seen as a weakness of character by many Greek men who drive with the patience and consideration of a 13 year old drug addict in need of a fix.

A few simple rules in case you are crazy enough to drive in Greece:

- You must always keep in mind that you may be the only person on the road who actually took and passed a proper driving test. Many Greek drivers simply bribed the people administering it. Just assume that nobody but you knows how to drive.
- The type of car you drive is considered to represent your status in the world.
- The bigger the car you drive, the more right of the way you have.
- Motorbikes don't obey any lanes or rules and there is usually one or more somewhere nearby. Watch out for them, especially on the islands where other tourists who have never driven a motorbike in their lives are doing so now and are possibly drunk too.
- Watch out for people parked in unbelievably stupid places, like when you come around a mountain bend and someone is relieving himself, or taking a picture of his girlfriend, while his car is parked halfway in the road.

- If you are given a lift don't try to wear your seatbelt. It is considered as lack of trust in the driver's driving ability, and it is likely you will be kicked out of the car.
- When asking directions expect to hear something like: Go about three kilometres, take a right at the traffic lights and ask someone else. Directions, no matter how precise, always include asking someone else.
- Young Greeks with nice cars drive fast. They do have excellent reflexes which gets them out of trouble as fast as they get into it, probably having something to do with a diet rich in caffeine and nicotine. That means you will have some close calls, almost guaranteed, but if you are attentive and they are not fighting with their girlfriend or mother on their mobile, chances are you won't have any major accidents. But they do happen.
- Fines are strict for breaking traffic laws in Greece but if you are caught breaking the law you can always try bribery. Most policemen are on the take anyway.
- If you are driving on a weekend, particularly on a Saturday evening or Sunday afternoon you should assume that everyone on the road except for you is drunk. Unless you are drunk too!
- In case I have discouraged you from driving and you have decided to walk everywhere, keep in mind that Greece also has one of the highest numbers of pedestrian deaths in the European Union.
- 'Zebra' crossings in Greece are mostly decorative, don't assume cars will stop.

GREEK NON-INSTITUTIONS

PRIVACY

Privacy is the only word from the English language that does not exists in the Greek language. There is no direct translation. The concept of 'privacy' is against the essence of being Greek. Greeks are not private people, if you are proud of who you – as most Greeks are - are why keep it to yourself? Greek people enjoy other peoples company and love passing opinion on everybody else's affairs, it is called 'constructive gossiping' ('koutsobolio'). It is a culture thing.

What a British person says:	What a Greek person hears:
'I am a private person'	I am lonely and sad
'I need my privacy'	I hate you
'I am on holiday alone'	I have no friends

THANK YOU', 'SORRY' AND 'EXCUSE ME'

In Greece someone who uses 'thank you' 'sorry' and excuse me' too often is considered gay or insincere, depending on their sex.

Greek people use 'thank you' and 'sorry' sparingly but they mean it! There is no corresponding word to 'excuse me'. 'Parakalo' (please) is the nearest (and more polite) equivalent.

> I once witnessed the use of 13 'thank you' (per person!) during a routine credit card payment. Disgusting!

THE HOUSING MARKET

The 'housing market' does not exist as a concept in Greece. Buying and selling houses is not common, especially as many houses do not have the correct property titles - they are built illegally. On the other hand, houses have a lot of character as they are specifically built, normally on land that the family has owned for generations, or maybe just bought after careful searching (sometimes for many years).

Land is relatively cheap so houses tend to be bigger than your average British house with large gardens so it is easy to extend. They are built on strong foundations with concrete as Greece and the surrounding area suffers from earthquakes.

HOMOSEXUALITY

There are no homosexual people in Greece. Homosexuality is simply not a Greek thing. To start with it is not a Greek word but a

Greek-Latin hybrid (that's a Greek word), coined by a German bloke in the 19th century who was fighting for homosexual rights. The actual word was 'homosexualität', and it was first seen in public print in 1869 when it appeared in two anonymous German pamphlets, and it was used alongside "normal sexual." These pamphlets were published as a method of fighting against the criminalization of homosexual sex in the newly formed federation of the northern German states. The earliest occurrence of 'homosexuality' in the Oxford English Dictionary was dated 1892. It entered the English language in the translation of 'Psychopathia Sexualis' by Richard Krafft-Ebing (just don't ask how I know so much about it).

From ancient times, Greeks have accepted Eros (Greek word) as a founding and fundamental force in Nature alongside Earth or Gaia (Greek word) and Chaos (Greek word). To confine Eros as something just between men and women is too restrictive and degenerating. Eros needs freedom so since ancient times, Greeks have no concept, no experience of 'homosexuality' and the modern division of sexual behaviour influenced by the Judeo-Christian-Muslim ideology (Greek word) has not changed that. Like other Mediterranean people, Greeks are mainly, obsessed with penises and what they do. It is not as big of a concern as to what exactly you do with it as long as you do something with it.

Paedophile is a word which has attracted bad publicity recently, but since it's Greek it is essentially good, so let me explain. Paedo- means kids, –phile, means friend of, as in euro-phile (friend of Europe), anglophile (friend of the English) and so on.
For example, Phil-ippos (as in Prince Phllip) means friend of horses (ippos). If you suggest that –phile means 'having sex with' is equivalent to suggesting that Prince Phillip is having sex with horses, that is plainly untrue. (It's Charles who is, isn't it?)A

Intimate relations between men were the bedrock of many ancient Greek societies. In ancient Crete, there were 'abductions' of lovers and wedding ceremonies between men, and there were laws about compulsory male-male relationships. Interestingly, the wedded boyfriends called each other 'brother', to argue for the non-lascivious character of those relationships. In Sparta homoerotic (Greek word) relationships between males had a public and official character. In Thebes close relations between the soldiers made the army stronger and led to the formation of the Sacred Band, an army consisting exclusively of male couples. In Athens during the classical age, Eros had no limits (well apart from one: age). Paedophilia is actually a Greek word, but all historic sources will agree it is not a Greek thing. The proof is in the beard. If the couple that seems intimate have beards they are men, ancient Greeks never shaved (Romans did), they liked the rough look. Eros is all about feelings and adoration. Certain sexual practises (Greek word) such as fellatio and anal sex were not common (and neither are Greek words, they are both Italian!)

Ancient Greeks thoughts constellations were evidence of Zeus's sperm hence 'Milky Way'. The most common sexual act for ancient Greek lovers was non-penetrative 'intercrural' (rubbing between the thighs) sometimes even with a cloak between the two bodies. This could only produce one result. When orgasm (Greek word) was reached, and the rubbing stopped, it left the rubbed one with a little constellation of his own. How innocent, how esoteric, how marvellous! Christianity changed the concept of intimate relations between men. Apparently God does not approve, but Greeks are still Greeks. Greek society nowadays has a somewhat hypocritical view to homosexuality, you are not considered homosexual if your intimate relations are not exclusive to men. If you are married, for example, but you have intimate affairs with men from time to time you are considered curious.

If you are not at the 'receiving end' of the love affair it is OK, you are not considered gay, either. Like ancient Greece it is only the passive sex that is frowned upon (but widely practised). Like in nearby Italy the one who does the penetrating is not considered gay, but the same cannot be said about the one who does the receiving.

STAND-UP COMEDY

Stand-up comedy (Greek word) is not something that exists in Greece, either. It is essentially an Anglo-Saxon thing that does not suit the Greek climate, character or society. There have been attempts to establish a stand-up comedy club, but they all failed miserably for a number of reasons.

Modern stand-up comedy consists of a person in an enclosed environment, essentially making fun of himself in a self-depreciating way and being critical (Greek word) of his surroundings and recent events. For the concept to work you need weather that makes you want to stay in, a person who is actually willing to stand on stage and talk to an audience, and an audience, who are willing to shut up and listen to this person and laugh with (or at) him and themselves. The audience keeps silent, apart from the laughing and the occasional heckling, because they do not want to attract attention to themselves and they are scared of being invited to come on stage to tell a better joke. None of this works in Greece or for Greeks (and many other cultures). There are only three to four months when staying in is better that being out, not long enough to base (Greek word) an industry on. We Greeks do not have much time for self-deprecation. You have to shout about how good you are to have any chance of being taken seriously. If you are modest you are probably not good.

A joke from Ancient Greece:
Someone said to Aristippos that his wife Laida (a very beautiful woman) does not love him, she only pretends to do so. Aristippos replied, "Neither wine nor fish love me, but I enjoy them."

Another joke from Ancient Greece:
A man says to his highly sexed wife, "What would you like to do? Eat or make love?"
"Whatever you like," she replied. "However, we don't have any bread."

And another joke from Ancient Greece:
A bald man swore at Diogenes. The philosopher replied, "I will not swear back at you. I will though, congratulate your hair for getting away from a stupid head."

The audience can also be a problem, attracting attention to yourself is not frowned upon, and in most cases it's sought after. With a Greek audience if a joke is good, the comedian will know about it, if it is bad he will also know about it. And at the first couple of not brilliant jokes most members of the audience would volunteer to come up and tell a better one, or start a monologue (Greek word) on how good they are at telling jokes. It's a nightmare. As I mentioned there have been a couple of attempts to start a comedy club in Athens, I was there. The wounds have not yet healed, neither the psychological (Greek word), nor the physical (Greek word).

Another limiting factor is the subjects that comedy can 'discuss'. The subject of Greece is out of the question, our mother country is too important. Family is also out of the question. If you joke about your family it is thought to be disrespectful ("Is this why your family raised you, to make jokes about them?" So the thinking goes). If it is about somebody else's family he better not be in the audience. And if he is not, it is thought cowardly to make jokes about them. You cannot joke about your mates either (they are your mates), or yourself: "What a sad 'malaka', he gets in front of strangers and tells jokes about himself!"

That leaves the politicians and other nations. Jokes about other nations are common – and stereotypical of course. As for the politicians who needs jokes when you have swearing!

Comedy is a (Greek word). It comes from the word 'komos' which in ancient times was a company of festive naked males dancing around a giant phallus (Greek word). It gives a whole new meaning to 'stand-up comedy'.

Some Greek Jokes:

A German, a Frenchman an Englishman and a Greek man are admiring a portrait of Adam and Eve in paradise. The German says, "Look at the perfection of their bodies. She is tall and slender and he is athletic with good muscles. They must be German." The Frenchman reacted immediately. "I don't think so. You can sense the sensuality from them both. They look so innocent yet they know the temptation is only around the corner. They must be French." "I am not sure," says the Englishman. "Look how relaxed they are. Look at the posture and the calmness of their movement. They can only be English." After a few moments of silence, the Greek man shouted, "I don't agree. They are both stark naked, they are sleeping under a tree, they are having a single apple for dinner and they think they are in paradise. They are Greek!"
A beggar nears a well dressed woman shopping in Kolonaki (a rich area in Athens) and says, "I have not eaten anything for four days." She replied, "Oh my God! I wish I had the will power to do this myself."
What do you call a bus that dances 'syrtaki'? Zor-bus

A Greek father calls his son a couple of days before Christmas and says, "Niko, I hate to ruin your holidays, but I must tell you that your mother and I are divorcing. Forty five years of misery is enough."

"Dad, what are you talking about?" Niko screams.

"We can't stand the sight of each other any longer, We're sick of each other, and I'm sick of talking about this, so you call your sister Toula and let her know."

Frantic, the son calls his sister who explodes on the phone. "No way are my loving parents getting divorced!" she shouts.

She calls Dad immediately and screams, "Dad, you are not getting divorced! Don't do anything until we get there. I'm calling Niko back and we'll be there tomorrow. Do you hear me?" and hangs up.

The old man hangs up his phone and turns to his wife. "OK," he says, "they're coming home for Christmas and paying their own way."

I came to Britain as a young, naïve, ouzo-drinking, mousaka loving macho Greek sex god and after 20 years I turned to a middle aged, ale worshiping, fish and chips addicted, alcoholic. I am fully integrated. Thank you Britain!

Image Permissions

Front Cover The Parthenon by Onkel Tuca!, CC BY-SA 3.0
Front Cover 0 Euro by Steve Balcombe
p24 Socrates by Eric Gaba, CC BY-SA-2.5
p40 Giorgios Papandreou by BartBassist CC BY-SA 2.0
p42 Angela Merkel by Armin Linnartz CC BY-SA 3.0 de
p44 Adolf Hitler by Bundesarchiv, CC BY-SA 3.0
p45 Dominique Strauss-Kahn, public domain
p61 The Acropolis by A. Savin, CC BY-SA 3.0
p61 The Parthenon by Steve Swayne, CC BY 2.0
p62 Parthenon Selene Horse by 3dnatureguy, CC BY-SA 3.0
p64 Nikos Kazantzakis by Kazantzakis Museum, CC BY 3.0
p65 Hippocrates, public domain
p67 Woman With Dildo by Sailko, CC BY 3.0
p68 Pythagoras by Galilea, CC BY-SA 3.0
p71 Zeus, public domain
p75 The Council Of Gods by Raphael, public domain

Special thanks to Anna, Mark, Louise, and especially Steve for all their help putting this guide together.
Dedicated to all my family.

"Manos offers a hysterically funny view of the Greek crisis"
Brighton Lite,

"Gentle, subtle humour and a splash of poetry... At times touching, other times amusing. Socrates would be proud."
Three Weeks

"Manos is very good. His humour extends to economics, etymology and couscous. And he has the only truly funny Susan Boyle joke I have heard"
Kate Copstick, The Scotsman

"Manos slickly plays up to the Greek stereotype. All the jokes you'd expect to hear about Greece are in: plate smashing, the Elgin Marbles, Turks, old ladies dressed in black, etc. It's very entertaining!"
Sappho Muses

Lightning Source UK Ltd.
Milton Keynes UK
UKOW06f0957250817
307892UK00007B/67/P

9 781905 691272